Listen Up!
LANGUAGE ARTS

Activities to Improve Language Arts and Listening Skills

by Ann Richmond Fisher
and Betsy Fisher

illustrated by Bron Smith

Teaching & Learning Company

1204 Buchanan St., P.O. Box 10
Carthage, IL 62321

Cover by Bron Smith

Copyright © 1995, Teaching & Learning Company

ISBN No. 1-57310-022-6

Printing No. 98765432

Teaching & Learning Company
1204 Buchanan St., P.O. Box 10
Carthage, IL 62321

This book belongs to

_____

Dedication

This book is lovingly dedicated
to Betsy's grandma and my mother-in-law,
Marilyn Fisher,
and to the memory of her late husband,
John Fisher.

Table of Contents

Dear Teacher,

This book is a resource you'll turn to over and over again as you practice those all-important language skills with your primary students. This is really two books in one—a *language arts* book that contains skills ranging from letter sounds to limericks and a *listening* book that stretches skills in hearing and following directions. As you use the lessons in this book, you are also enhancing students' language and listening abilities simultaneously. (No one needs to tell you, the classroom teacher, how important it is to teach good listening habits and yet how difficult it is to take time away from content areas to do it!)

This book is designed to be a complete resource for the busy teacher. It contains everything from pretests to an answer key. The lessons were also written to be easy to use. For many of the lessons, students will need only a piece of paper and a pencil. For others they may need crayons or a reproducible page. An answer key is provided in the back of the book which will often help you check students' work at a glance.

The language lessons are arranged by topic as listed in the table of contents. In general, easier lessons are placed first in each section. The skill covered is also listed at the top of each lesson for your quick reference. It is suggested that you begin with easier lessons that contain information with which your students are already comfortable so that the focus at first will be on listening. You may also want to repeat directions two or three times in the beginning and then gradually move towards both harder skills and less teacher help.

The section that follows, "How to Use This Book," contains more specific instructions on using special features of the book such as the Pre/Posttests and Warm-Ups. It is our goal to help you improve the listening skills of your students in an easy, enjoyable manner!

Sincerely,

Ann *Betsy*

Ann Richmond Fisher and Betsy Fisher

How to Use This Book

To get maximum benefit from the various features of this book, use the suggestions that follow.

Warm-Ups: These are fun activities at the beginning of each section that will introduce students to the upcoming content area. The purpose of the warm-ups is not only to give students a sample of the work ahead but also to get students excited about it.

Pre/Posttests: These have been written to help the teacher evaluate student progress. The teacher should carefully preview the upcoming unit before administering the pretest. If some lessons are inappropriate for your class (i.e. too difficult or too easy), then there may also be inappropriate items on the pre/posttest. Feel free to use only the questions on the tests that correspond to lessons in the unit you will actually be using. Come up with your own number for the highest possible test score. Use the **Teacher Record Page** to record the date of each pretest, the number of items on the test and each student's score. After the class completes all appropriate lessons in the unit, administer the same test again, and again record student scores for the posttest on the record page. At a glance you can see which students are making significant progress in their listening and language skills. If some students are not improving, try to work with them individually or in small groups to diagnose any problems they may be having.

Lessons: Most lessons are written so that you can read them to an entire class while each student completes one page of work. You can then collect the work and evaluate it using the **Answer Key** in the back of the book. Or students can check their own work as the entire class works through the correct solution together. IMPORTANT: In each lesson students are instructed where to write their names on the paper. Make sure they wait and listen to these instructions. Also note that for some lessons such as "Animal Action" (page 42) and "Dictated Rhymes" (page 61), students' answers will vary from the sample solutions given.

Although the lessons can be administered in a traditional manner described above, some can also be adapted to other formats. A few ideas are listed below. Feel free to use your imagination and try other ideas of your own.

Classroom Brainstorming: Some lessons such as "Think!" (page 38), "Animal Action" (page 42) and "Dictated Rhymes" (page 61) can be conducted orally. Encourage students to supply as many sensible answers as possible. Don't list words on chalkboard (if you want a list for future use, write it on paper instead) so that students are required to listen to others' responses. Challenge students to give as many reasonable solutions as possible without duplicating previous answers.

Cooperative Learning Groups: Some of the lessons (especially the more difficult ones) can be solved in small groups. Students will need to agree on what they've heard and then work together to come up with solutions. "Scrambled Sense 1 and 2" (pages 25-26), "Synonym Stories" (page 32) and "Capital Sentences" (page 52) are some lessons you may choose to conduct in this way.

Chalkboard Lessons: "Write the Letter" (page 7), "Vowel Votes" (page 13), "Puppy Love" (page 76) and several others written on plain paper can also be done at the chalkboard. You may wish to have three or four students at the board while the rest of the students work at their seats. This allows you to spot problems immediately and helps you know how to pace the instructions. The chalkboard workers may be distracting to the other students; they will need to listen and concentrate even harder. They may need to be reminded that other answers may be possible, or that some answers may be incorrect. Emphasize the need for each child to do his own best work.

Team Relays: Some activities could be done at the board by teams of four to six students working in a relay fashion. "Hidden Opposites" (page 31), "Not a Noun" (page 44) and others could be done in this manner. One member from each team would go to the chalkboard and answer one item, the next member would do the next item, etc. Along the way, other team members would need to be sure they agreed on the correct answer. One person from each team could be given the opportunity to correct earlier mistakes.

Teacher Record Page

Student Name	# possible	Pretest 1	Posttest 1	Pretest 2	Posttest 2	Pretest 3	Posttest 3	Pretest 4	Posttest 4	Pretest 5	Posttest 5	Pretest 6	Posttest 6
Date													

Materials:
*Reproducible on page 2
Crayons: green, orange*

Letters and Letter Sounds

1. Look at the letters in row 1. Find the letter *D*. Put a green *X* on it. Find the letter *F*. Circle it with your orange crayon.

2. Look at the letters in row 2. Listen to the **N** sound. You hear the **N** sound in *nut, Nancy, nickel* and *November*. Find the letter that makes the **N** sound and put an orange *X* on it. Listen to the **L** sound and underline the letter that makes it with your green crayon. Some words that start with the **L** sound are *little, light, lamp* and *laugh*.

3. In box 3, use your green crayon to write the letter you hear at the beginning of these words: *grin, guitar, glove* and *guest*.

4. In box 4, using your green crayon, write the letter you hear at the beginning of these words: *water, worm, wasp* and *winter*.

5. In box 5, make one tally mark for each time you hear the **R** sound in this sentence: Ruth wrote Rick a letter.

6. In box 6, make one tally mark each time you hear the **P** sound in this sentence: I hope that Patty likes my purple plum pie.

7. Look at the pictures in row 7. Three of the names of these pictures begin with the same sound. Listen to the words: *bug, bat, dog* and *bone*. Circle the three pictures that begin with the same sound. Only one of the words has a long vowel sound. Put an *X* on the picture of the word with a long vowel sound. Listen to the words again: *bug, bat, dog* and *bone*.

8. In row 8, each of these words is missing a vowel. I will say each completed word, and you will add the missing vowel. Here are the words: *step, mop* and *tan*.

9. I will read four words to you. Listen carefully to see how many have a short **I**. Write that number (1, 2, 3 or 4) in the blank by number 9. Words: *pig, will, rag* and *hen*.

10. Write your name under number 9.

ABCDEFG...OH, BABY, BABY...

Letters and Letter Sounds

1. A   B   C   D   E   F   G

2. H   I   J   K   L   M   N

3. ☐   4. ☐   5. ☐   6. ☐

7.

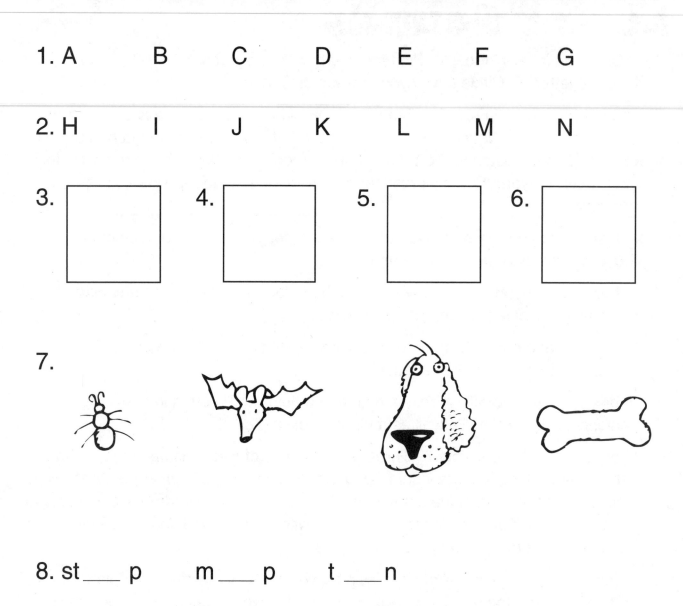

8. st ___ p   m ___ p   t ___ n

9. _____

Skills:
Recognizing begin-
ning sounds

Materials:
Just students

Stand Up, Sit Down

Use this page as a Warm-Up for Part 1.

I am going to say several pairs of words for you. If the two words have the *same* beginning sound, stand up. If the two words have *different* beginning sounds, sit down.

1. party, peacock
2. bubble, bath
3. apple, stop
4. happy, hunt
5. vase, bag

6. rattle, wrinkle
7. cut, paste
8. deer, dig
9. jump, sand
10. shell, shadow

11. circle, sun
12. grass, green
13. blue, red
14. think, thick
15. friend, free

16. funny, sad
17. walk, water
18. clock, flash
19. check, chill
20. tickle, shake

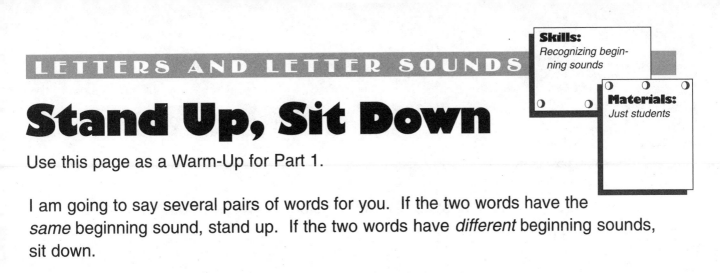

End Action

Skills:
Recognizing ending
sounds

Materials:
Just students

Now let's listen for ending sounds. If the two words I read have the *same* ending sound, clap your hands once. If the two words have *different* ending sounds, stomp your foot once. Now let's stand in a circle while we listen to these words.

1. pig, flag
2. snow, rain
3. seat, note
4. book, read

5. box, tricks
6. pass, bus
7. teach, slug
8. calf, cow

9. doll, bell
10. kick, sock
11. band, sing
12. path, with

13. sled, man
14. same, zoom
15. tip, tock
16. rich, peach

Skills: Identifying letters of the alphabet

Materials: Reproducible on page 5
Crayons: red, blue, green, yellow, orange

Find the Letter

(Teacher: You may choose to specify that your students mark just the uppercase letter, just the lowercase letter or both.)

1. Find the letter *P*. Circle it with your blue crayon.
2. Find the letter *C*. Underline it with your orange crayon.
3. Find the letter *S*. Circle it with your green crayon.
4. Find the letter *K*. Underline it with your yellow crayon.
5. Find the letter *O*. Put a blue *X* on it.
6. Find the letter *A*. Circle it with your red crayon.
7. Find the letter *W*. Circle it with your yellow crayon.
8. Find the letter *E*. Put an orange box around it.
9. Find the letter *J*. Underline it with your blue crayon.
10. Find the letter *N*. Put a red dot above it.
11. Find the letter *Z*. Write your name next to it with your green crayon.
12. Find the letter *B*. Put a green box around it.
13. Find the letter *H*. Put a yellow *X* on it.
14. Find the letter *F*. Circle it with your orange crayon.
15. Find the letter *Y*. Underline it with your green crayon.
16. Find the letter *M*. Put a red box around it.
17. Find the letter *T*. Put a blue dot above it.
18. Find the letter *I*. Draw a yellow box around it.
19. Find the letter *X*. Put a green dot above it.
20. Find the letter *Q*. Put a red *X* on it.
21. Find the letter *V*. Put an orange dot above it.
22. Find the letter *L*. Put an orange *X* on it.
23. Find the letter *R*. Put a blue box around it.
24. Find the letter *D*. Put a green *X* on it.
25. Find the letter *U*. Put a yellow dot above it.
26. Find the letter *G*. Put two red lines under it.

ABC Chart

Reproducible for use with pages 4 and 6.

Aa Bb Cc Dd

Ee Ff Gg Hh

Ii Jj Kk Ll

Mm Nn Oo Pp

Qq Rr Ss Tt

Uu Vv Ww Xx

Yy Zz

Skills:
Identifying consonant sounds: b, d, f, h, l, m, n, p, r, t

Materials:
Reproducible on page 5
Crayons: brown, blue, orange, green

LETTERS AND LETTER SOUNDS

Letter Sounds

1. Listen to the sound **B**. Do you know what letter makes that sound? Find the letter on your worksheet, and circle it with your brown crayon. Here are some words that begin with the **B** sound: *baby, bone, Bobby, bill* and *bubble.*

2. Listen to the sound **T**. Find the letter that makes the **T** sound and underline it with your brown crayon. Here are some words that begin with the **T** sound: *table, talk, tiny* and *tiptoe.*

3. Listen to the **D** sound. You hear it in *Daddy, dinner, dark, dinosaur* and *dentist.* Find the letter that makes the **D** sound, and circle it with your orange crayon.

4. Listen to the sound **R**. Find the letter that makes the **R** sound, and underline it with your orange crayon. Some **R** words are *rabbit, rock, riddle, radish* and *rug.*

5. Listen to the sound **F**. Find the letter that makes the **F** sound, put an *X* on it with your blue crayon. Some words that start with the **F** sound are *fish, fun, fair, fiddle* and *fence.*

6. Listen to the **P** sound. Find the letter that makes the **P** sound, and circle it with your blue crayon. Some words that start with the **P** sound are *pop, party, pencil, pull* and *pickle.*

7. Listen to the **N** sound. You hear the **N** sound in *nut, Nancy, nickel* and *November.* Find the letter that makes the **N** sound, and put an orange *X* on it.

8. Listen to the sound **H**. Find the letter that makes the **H** sound, and circle it with your blue crayon. Here are some **H** words that begin with the **H** sound: *happy, hop, help, hope* and *huddle.*

9. Listen to the sound **L**. Find the letter that makes the **L** sound, and underline it with your green crayon. Some words that start with the **L** sound are *little, light, lamp, laugh* and *lettuce.*

10. Listen to the **M** sound. Find the letter that makes the **M** sound, and put a green *X* on it. Some words that start with the **M** sound are *monkey, milk, mat, mail* and *mess.*

(Teacher: This exercise can be varied with the use of other sounds. In this lesson, we have avoided sounds like **S** and **K** that can be spelled with more than one letter.)

Write the Letter

Skills:
Identifying the letters f, g, j, u, w, y and z by their sounds
Writing letters left and right

Materials:
Blank paper
Pencil
Crayons

Fold your paper in half the long way so you have a left half and a right half. Flatten your paper out. Now fold it in half crosswise, crease it and flatten it back out. You should have two boxes on the top of your paper and two boxes on the bottom half of your paper, or four boxes altogether on the front of your paper and four boxes on the back. Find the box on the front of your paper that is in the top left corner. At the top of this box, write your name. Draw a picture of something that starts with the same letter as your name.

Now move to the box that is in the top right corner. I will name several objects. Write the letter in this box that you hear at the beginning of all these words: *fish, fat, furniture, fuzz, film* and *fine*.

Next, go to the box in the bottom left corner. Write the letter in this box that you hear at the beginning of all these words: *zebra, zipper, zinnia, zucchini* and *zero*.

Now go to the last box on the front of your paper. Write the letter in this box that you hear at the beginning of all these words: *unicorn, unicycle, United States* and *ukulele*.

Now turn your paper over. Find the box in the top left corner. Write the letter in this box that you hear at the beginning of all these words: *guitar, guest, gourd, goose* and *gum*.

Now go to the bottom left box. Write the letter in this box that you hear at the beginning of these words: *water, watermelon, worm, wasp* and *winter*.

Next move to the top right box. Write the letter in this box that you hear at the beginning of these words: *jeep, jet, jelly, jam* and *jail*.

Finally, move to the last box on the back of your paper. Write the letter in this box that you hear at the beginning of these words: *yard, yarn, yeast, yo-yo* and *yam*.

Now go back over your paper. Add a small picture to each box of something that begins with the letter that you have written. You may draw one of the objects I named or think of one of your own.

Skills:
Listening for spe-
cific
sounds

Materials:
Lined paper
Pencil

LETTERS AND LETTER SOUNDS

Sentence Sounds

Write your name at the top of your paper. Number your paper from 1 to 12. For each number, I will read a sentence. I want you to count how many times you hear a certain letter sound in the sentence. By each number, make a tally mark each time you hear the sound.

As an example, let's do number 1 together. The letter I want you to listen for is the **B** sound. Here is the sentence: Ben bought a bike. You would make three tally marks by the number 1 because in the first sentence you heard the **B** sound three times: *Ben, bought* and *bike.*

Now let's go on to the rest. Listen carefully, because sometimes the sound might be in the middle or at the end of a word.

2. Listen for the **K** sound. Sentence: Keith keeps his keys in his pocket. (Repeat sentence slowly each time.)

3. Listen for the **S** sound. Sentence: Sally can't come out, so maybe Sammy or Sarah can.

4. Listen for the **T** sound. Sentence: Tim and Tina will get into town today.

5. Listen for the **N** sound. Sentence: Now Nick needs a nickel.

6. Listen for the **R** sound. Sentence: Ruth wrote Rick a letter.

7. Listen for the **M** sound. Sentence: Monkeys might make a mess in my room.

8. Listen for the **P** sound. Sentence: I hope that Patty likes my pink plum pie.

9. Listen for the **J** sound. Sentence: Jack and Jill like jam and jelly.

10. Listen for the **Z** sound. Sentence: Zip up your coat before you buzz around in the blizzard.

11. Listen for the **D** sound. Sentence: Do you dance in red, shiny dancing shoes?

12. Listen for the **F** sound. Sentence: Find out how Fatima fell off the roof.

Picture This!

Skills:
Recognizing same and different beginning sounds

Materials:
Reproducible on page 10
Pencil

1. Write your name at the top of your paper.

2. Find the row of pictures that has a bug in it. Listen to the names of all the objects in this row as I say them for you: *bug, bat, dog* and *bone*. Three of the words all begin with the same sound. Can you tell what sound it is and which are the three words? Listen again: *bug, bat, dog* and *bone*. When you've found the three that start with the same sound, circle those three pictures.

3. Now find the row of pictures with the mask. Listen to the names of the pictures in this row: *mask, mitt, moon* and *cake*. Which one begins with a sound that is different from the other three? When you find it, put an *X* on it. The words again are *mask, mitt, moon* and *cake*.

4. Next find the row of pictures that begins with the vase. Here are the names of all the pictures in the row: *vase, vine, vest* and *rake*. Find the three pictures that begin with the same sound. Circle them. I will say their names again: *vase, vine, vest* and *rake*.

5. Now find the row of pictures with the rat. Listen to the names of all the pictures in this row: *rat, elf, robe* and *rose*. Three of the words all begin with the same sound, but one has a different beginning sound. Find the picture with a different beginning sound, and put an *X* on it. I'll say the words again for you: *rat, elf, robe* and *rose*.

6. Now find the row of pictures with the cup. Listen to the names of all the pictures in this row: *cup, duck, cake* and *comb*. Which three begin with the same sound? Find the three pictures and circle them. Here are the pictures' names again: *cup, duck, cake* and *comb*.

7. Lastly, find the row of pictures that has the tree in it. Listen to the names of all the objects in this row as I say them for you: *tree, pig, pie* and *puppy*. Which picture begins with a sound that is different from the other three words? When you've found the one that's different, put an *X* on that picture. The words again are *tree, pig, pie* and *puppy*.

Rows of Pictures

Reproducible for use with pages 9 and 11.

Skills:
Hearing long and
short vowel sounds

Materials:
Reproducible on
page 10
Pencil

Long and Short

1. Find the row with the mask in it. You will see a mask, mitt, moon and cake. Find the word with a short **I** sound like you hear in *his*. Circle it. Find the picture with a long **A** sound like you hear in *ape*. Underline it.

2. Find the row with the rat. There is a rat, elf, robe and rose. Two of these words have the long **O** sound like you hear in *hope*. Find those two pictures and circle them. Find the picture with a short **E** sound as in *bed*. Draw a box around it.

3. Find the row with the bug. You will see a bug, bat, dog and bone. Only one of these words has a long vowel sound. Can you find it? Circle the picture with a long vowel sound. Underline the picture with the short **O** sound like you hear in *hot*.

4. Look at the row that begins with a vase. You will see a vase, vine, vest and rake. Two words have a long **A** sound like you hear in *cage*. Find those two pictures and underline them. Only one picture in the row has a short vowel sound. Circle that picture.

5. Look at the row with the cup, duck, cake and comb. Two words have the short **U** sound that you hear in *rug*. Find them and circle them. Find the picture with the long **O** sound like you hear in *rope* and underline it.

6. Find the row of pictures that begins with the tree. In this row are a tree, pig, pie and puppy. Two of these words contain long vowel sounds. Underline those two pictures. One word in this row has the short **U** sound like you hear in *dug*. Circle that picture.

7. Write your name at the bottom of the page.

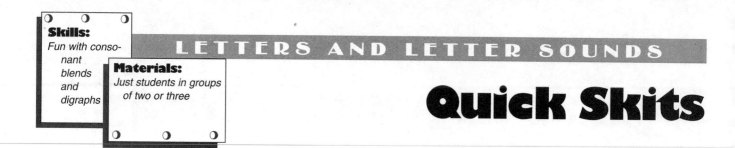

Skills:
Fun with consonant blends and digraphs

Materials:
Just students in groups of two or three

Quick Skits

You will be working in your group to act out three words that begin with the same consonant blend. I will come around to your group and whisper your three words to you *one* time. You then need to figure out a quick way to pantomime (act out without speaking) these words for the rest of the class. The other groups will watch your three skits, and then discuss together what the words and the blend might be. After a minute or two of discussion, I will call on one of the groups to see if they've figured out your answer.

Blends and words to assign:

1. gr: grip, grind, grasshopper
2. sh: shake, shoulder, shin
3. th: think, thorn, thirty
4. bl: blow, blink, blouse
5. fr: fruit, freckle, Frisbee™
6. tr: train, trash, trip
7. cr: crab, crocodile, crush
8. dr: dress, drum, drive
9. wr: wrist, write, wreath
10. pl: play, plum, please

11. st: stamp, stink, stick
12. gl: glad, glue, glove
13. br: braid, brush, breathe
14. thr: three, throat, threw
15. pr: pray, prance, present
16. cl: clock, clip, class
17. fl: flower, fly, flip
18. ch: chicken, chop, chuckle
19. str: string, stretch, strong
20. sl: sleeve, slow, sleep

(Teacher: You may want to keep score to add to the competition. Have each group write down their guess for the others' blends. Then award each group that finds the right blend one point each time. Also award each group two points for every group that guesses their act correctly. Total points at the end of the activity.)

CLUCK!
CLUCK!
CLUCK!

Skills:
*Identifying short
vowel sounds*

Materials:
Blank paper
Pencil

Vowel Votes

Put the letters *a, e* and *i* on the chalkboard. Show students how to divide
their papers into three columns with one letter at the top of each column. Also instruct
them on how to make tally marks, if necessary.

You now have three columns on your paper, each with a different vowel at the top.
When I read a word, I want you to listen to it carefully and decide which short vowel it
uses in the middle of the word. When you think you know which vowel it is, give that
vowel, "vote" by making a tally mark in that vowel's column. For example: If I said the
word *rat*, would you know where to put your vote? That's right, in the **a** column. Now
let's begin.

1. bed	6. ham	11. rag	16. lad
2. pig	7. sit	12. hen	17. pen
3. hat	8. cat	13. pet	18. net
4. will	9. bell	14. pan	19. pin
5. leg	10. mitt	15. lid	20. men

Now count the number of votes for each vowel. Write your name in the column that
has the most votes.

Teacher: Here is an alternate word list for using the short vowels *i, o* and *u.*

1. hot	6. pit	11. bus	16. cup
2. nut	7. run	12. kit	17. hut
3. win	8. hop	13. shot	18. fin
4. sun	9. rim	14. mop	19. not
5. lock	10. cud	15. bit	20. rug

Skills:
Filling in missing vowels

Materials:
Reproducible on page 15
Pencil

LETTERS AND LETTER SOUNDS

Missing Vowels

Write your name at the top of the page. In this lesson, you will see twenty words, each with a missing letter. The letter that is missing is a vowel. Each one on this page has the short sound. I will say each word for you, then you need to complete the word with the correct vowel. Listen carefully so you can decide which vowel goes in each blank. I will write the vowels on the board now so you can look at them if you need to. (Write *a, e, i, o* and *u* on the board.)

1. vest
2. stop
3. step
4. skit
5. dad
6. cut
7. did
8. cot
9. skill
10. pat

11. mutt
12. bun
13. yet
14. sat
15. mop
16. went
17. tan
18. kin
19. hut
20. top

14

Missing Vowels

Reproducible for use with page 14.

1. v ___ st

2. st ___ p

3. st ___ p

4. sk ___ t

5. d ___ d

6. c ___ t

7. d ___ d

8. c ___ t

9. sk ___ ll

10. p ___ t

11. m ___ tt

12. b ___ n

13. y ___ t

14. s ___ t

15. m ___ p

16. w ___ nt

17. t ___ n

18. k ___ n

19. h ___ t

20. t ___ p

Spelling and Vocabulary

Write your name in the top right corner of your paper. Number your paper from 1 to 10.

For the first three items, I will say a word, spell it and say it again. You need to listen carefully to hear if I spell the word correctly. If I do, put a *Y* for *yes* by the number. If I do not spell the word correctly, put an *N* for *no* by the number.

1. that–THAT–that
2. jab–CAB–jab
3. grass–GRAS–grass

For the next two items, pretend that I am from another planet called Fluton. A lot of objects on Fluton are like things you have on Earth, but they are called by a different name. I will describe something for you, and then I will give you three choices. You choose which thing on Earth is like what I've talked about.

4. Googles fall out of the sky. They are icy cold and melt when they touch my warm skin. What are googles? Put the letter of the right answer. Here are three choices: a. acorns, b. raindrops, c. snowflakes. Put your answer–a., b., c.–by the number 4 on your paper.

5. For fun on Fluton, children like to play Umtoe. Umtoe is a great game because you need only two people to play it, and you can play it outside on a table or if it's raining, you can play it inside on a table or on the floor. What game is Umtoe like? Here are your three choices: a. baseball, b. checkers, c. hockey. Write the letter of your answer by number 5.

For the next two items, you will also have three choices for the right answer. I will read a sentence, leaving out the last word. From the choices I give you, select the one that makes the most sense in the sentence.

6. Today the sky is clear and ____ . Your choices are a. blue, b. blow, c. shoes. Write the letter of your answer by the number 6 on your paper.

7. For dessert, I'll have some lemon ____ . Choose: a. get, b. cake, c. sun.

For the last three items, I will read some letters which you need to write on the line next to each number. Then I will read you the meaning of a word. Try to unscramble the letters to spell a word that fits the meaning I have given you. Write the new word on the line next to the letters.

8. G-I-N-K: Spell a word that is the name of a man who rules over a country.

9. L-Y-A-P: Spell a word that tells what you do with your toys.

10. B-L-A-T-E: Spell the name of a piece of furniture.

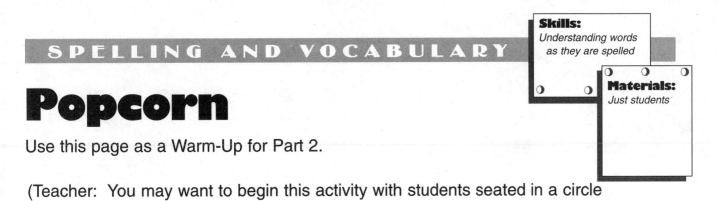

Popcorn

Use this page as a Warm-Up for Part 2.

(Teacher: You may want to begin this activity with students seated in a circle on the floor.)

In this activity I am going to spell the name of an animal. As soon as you know what word I've spelled, you may "pop" out of your seat, say the animal name and act like that animal. For example: If I say the letters *C, A, T*, you will stand up and say, "Cat" and start meowing.

1. B A T
2. P I G
3. A P E
4. G O A T
5. F O X

6. D O G
7. O W L
8. C O W
9. R A T
10. D U C K

11. S H E E P
12. F I S H
13. L I O N
14. T U R T L E
15. B E A R

16. T I G E R
17. H I P P O
18. H O R S E
19. R A B B I T
20. C R A B

Skills:
Listening for correct spelling

Materials:
Blank paper
Pencil

SPELLING AND VOCABULARY

Is It Right?

Write your name at the top of your paper. Number your paper from 1 to 12. In this lesson I will say a word, spell it and say it again. You need to listen carefully to hear if I spell the word correctly. If I spell the word correctly, put a *Y* for *yes* by the number. If the word is not spelled correctly, put an *N* for *no*. (Teacher: You may want to do the first one together.)

1. that–THAT–that

Now let's go on to the rest. Listen carefully to hear if I spell the word correctly.

2. tab–TIB–tab

3. grass–GRAS–grass

4. yap–YAP–yap

5. skunk–SKUK–skunk

6. ten–TEN–ten

7. ring–INRG–ring

8. ranch–RANCH–ranch

9. chum–UMCH–chum

10. jab–CAB–jab

11. wax–WAK–wax

12. bank–BANK–bank

(Teacher: You could adapt this lesson frequently to include the week's spelling words.)

ah, HeRe IT IS...
S...K...U...n...K !

Fluton's Follies

Skills:
Finding the meaning of nonsense words from context clues

Materials:
*Reproducible on page 21
Crayons: red, blue, yellow, green*

Pretend that I am from another planet. I've come to visit Earth to tell you about my planet and to learn about yours. On your paper you can see some objects that we have on my planet, Fluton. These objects are a lot like things you have on Earth, but they go by different names. I am going to describe objects with their Fluton names. You need to listen carefully to decide which Earth thing is like what I'm describing. Then I will give you some directions to mark the objects. You will not use every picture on the page, and you will not use any object more than once. Write your name at the top of your paper.

1. The first thing I will tell you about are googles. Googles fall out of the sky. They are icy cold and melt when they touch my warm skin. What are googles? Find a picture of them and circle them with your blue crayon.

2. On Fluton we have zotos. Zotos always come in pairs–a left one and a right one. We wear them on parts of our bodies; in fact, we wear them on our zimboes to keep our zimboes warm and to protect them from stones and other sharp objects that we might walk on. Can you guess what these zotos are that we wear on our zimboes? Find them and circle them with your red crayon.

3. Something we eat on Fluton is called a jumple. A jumple is healthy, crispy and delicious. It grows on trees. With it we make pie, sauce and juice. Find the jumple on your page and circle it with your yellow crayon.

4. On Fluton we like to ride on a thunk. A thunk is very easy to get around on. It doesn't use any gasoline because it doesn't have an engine. Young people can ride it by themselves (as long as they are careful) because they don't need a driver's license to use it. Find the object that must be like a thunk. Underline it with your red crayon.

5. For fun on Fluton, children like to play Umtoe. Umtoe is a great game because you need only two people to play it, and you can play it outside on a table or if it's raining, you can play it inside on a table or on the floor. Find the things you would need to play Umtoe. Circle them with your green crayon.

6. Most people on Fluton own a lot of quozats. If you are all alone and a little bored, a quozat can be good company. You can read a quozat and learn all about a new person or place. A quozat can help your imagination have new adventures. A quozat can be happy, sad, mysterious, helpful or even funny. Find the picture of a quozat and underline it with your blue crayon.

Fluton's Follies

7. On Fluton, most families have a koob in their living room. They use their koob when they want to relax. The nice thing about a koob is that several people can sit together while they talk or read a story. If only one person wants to use a koob, he can really stretch out and rest. Find the koob and put a yellow line under it.

8. Many people on Fluton like to keep powgies for pets. Powgies have long ears and soft fur. They like to eat crunchy orange vegetables. When they get out of their cage, they like to hop. Find the powgie and put a green line under it.

9. Most families on Fluton own only one figgle. Figgles are very expensive on Fluton, and since most people can walk to work or school, they don't need one as much as you might. Another problem we have with figgles is that the tires are very hard to change. If we had to change all four tires at once, it could take us a week to do it! Find the figgle and put a blue X on it.

10. An unusual habit we have on Fluton is that we wear our chims every day of the year. Here you only wear them when it's cold outside, but on Fluton we find that wearing them helps drown out some of the noise on our planet caused by all the crackling and popping that comes from our air. I know it sounds strange, but on Fluton our air is noisy, and the chims help to protect our ears. Many of us have several different chims so we don't get tired of wearing the same ones every day. Can you find a picture of our chims? Put a yellow X on the picture.

11. Another strange thing is that on Earth you eat valeems. On Fluton, we put them under our pillow! You find that they are healthy, crunchy food, especially good for your eyesight. We find that putting the long and hard valeems under our pillows keeps us from getting kinks in our long, lumpy necks! Find the valeem. Put a red X on it.

12. Finally, let me tell you about our zutes. Our zutes make the most beautiful music heard anywhere in the universe. We take lessons to learn how to play them just like you do. The keys on yours are black and white, but on our zutes they are orange and purple. Find the zute and put a green X on it.

Fluton's Follies

Reproducible for use with pages 19 and 20.

Skills:
Choosing the word that makes sense

Materials:
Reproducible on page 23
Pencil

SPELLING AND VOCABULARY

Three Choices

In this lesson, you can see three words in each line. I will read a sentence for each group of words, and you need to circle the word that makes sense in the sentence. For example, by number 1 the words are *big, eat* and *dog*. The sentence is Rover is my pet _____ . Which word makes sense? That's right, the word *dog*. Circle the word *dog*. Now let's work on the other sentences.

2. I live in a yellow _____ .

3. Would you like to _____ in my chair?

4. This is my favorite library _____ .

5. For dessert, I'll have some lemon _____ .

6. I cannot _____ to the party.

7. A lot of rain will make the grass nice and _____ .

8. The clothes in the washer are _____ .

9. Sally left early because she did not feel _____ .

10. Tim is in the second grade _____ .

11. Today the sky is clear and _____ .

12. Miss Sanchez will _____ the book to her class.

13. I would like you to come _____ , please.

14. Yesterday, I _____ a deer run across the field.

15. Write your name in the top right corner of your page.

Three Choices

Reproducible for use with page 23.

1. big	eat	dog
2. run	stop	house
3. car	sit	no
4. book	red	went
5. cake	sun	get
6. good	cut	go
7. hat	green	and
8. wet	am	here
9. yellow	this	well
10. the	class	are
11. blue	blow	shoe
12. come	read	fun
13. me	store	here
14. saw	then	was

Skills:
Correct spelling

Materials:
*Just students, divided
into two teams*

SPELLING AND VOCABULARY

Team Spell

Line up two spelling teams as you would for a spelldown. Pronounce the word to be spelled for the first team. The first member of the team says the first letter, the second person gives the second letter, etc. The next student in line after the word is finished has the opportunity to correct any letters already given. After that student is done, award a point to the team if the final word was spelled correctly. Award no point if the final word was incorrect. Pronounce a new word to the second team and follow the same procedure.

This format requires students to listen not only to the teacher as the word is pronounced but also to other students as the word is spelled.

Variations:

1. Have the team members come to the board and write the letter they are adding to the word. (This reduces the need to listen but may be helpful for younger students.)

2. Award two points if a team spells the word correctly without making any changes; award one point if the team spells the word correctly after making changes.

Word lists vary with the ability of your class. Here are two possible word lists.

First Grade		Second Grade	
after	help	always	inch
any	house	around	just
ask	like	best	know
by	may	black	many
cat	off	could	read
did	open	does	right
eat	pretty	every	sack
from	push	first	small
going	put	found	something
good	red	goes	their
green	stop	great	there
has	town	hitch	would

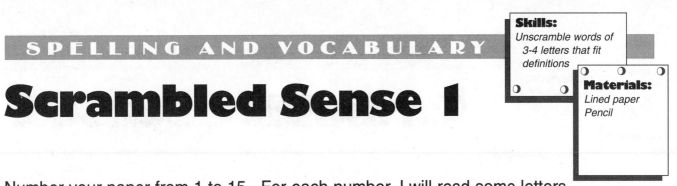

Scrambled Sense 1

Skills:
Unscramble words of
3-4 letters that fit
definitions

Materials:
Lined paper
Pencil

Number your paper from 1 to 15. For each number, I will read some letters. You need to write these letters on the line next to the number. Then I will read you the meaning of a word. Look at the letters you have written down, and try to unscramble them to spell a word that fits the meaning I have given you. Write the new word next to the scrambled letters.

1. (Do this one together.) A-P-N: Spell a word that is something you can use for cooking.

2. G-I-N-K: Spell a word that is the name of a man who rules over a country.

3. M-U-R-D: Spell a word that is the name of an instrument that you play by hitting with sticks.

4. C-P-L-A: Spell a word that tells how you can make a sound by putting your hands together.

5. F-I-G-T Spell a word that names a present you could give someone.

6. E-T-N: Spell a word that is used to catch insects or fish.

7. E-T-N: Use these same letters to spell a number word.

8. X-I-F: Spell a word that means to repair something.

9. A-P-M: Spell a word of something you look at to find directions to get someplace.

10. L-Y-A-P: Spell a word that tells what you do with your toys.

11. D-R-E: Spell a color word.

12. C-P-U: Spell something you can use for drinking.

13. B-C-K-A: Spell a word that is the opposite of *front*.

14. P-O-T-S: Spell a word that is the opposite of *go*.

15. Write your name on this line.

SPELLING AND VOCABULARY

Scrambled Sense 2

Follow the same directions as on the previous page. These words are a little longer and therefore, a little more difficult.

1. S-G-N-I-T: Spell a word that tells what you might get from a bee.

2. S-A-S-C-L: Spell a word that names a group of students.

3. S-H-A-L-S-P: Spell a word that tells a sound you might make when you dive into water.

4. B-N-C-H-U: Spell a word that names a group of grapes.

5. C-T-C-H-A: Spell a word that tells something you can do with a baseball.

6. C-H-R-B-A-N: Spell a word that names part of a tree.

7. K-N-U-R-T: Spell a word that names a different part of a tree.

8. C-O-L-K-C: Spell a word that helps you with time.

9. N-E-C-I-L-P: Spell a word that tells what you use for writing.

10. L-O-Y-E-W-L: Spell a color word.

11. G-T-E-H-I: Spell a number word.

12. B-L-A-T-E: Spell the name of a piece of furniture.

13. S-E-R-H-O: Spell the name of an animal.

14. S-I-H-R-T: Spell the name of something you could wear.

15. D-A-L-S-A: Spell something that is healthy to eat.

16. Write your name under your last word.

Materials:
Lined paper
Pencil

Antonyms, Synonyms and Homonyms

Write your name at the top of your paper. Number from 1 to 12.
For numbers 1 and 2, I will read you two words. If they mean the same, write *S*. If they have opposite meanings, write *O*.

1. open, close
2. dirty, soiled

For number 3, I will read you part of a silly story. Make tally marks to show how many things the girl, Opal Opposite, does that are backwards or opposite from the way you would normally do them.

3. At bedtime, Opal remembered to wash her face and brush her *toes*. Then to make sure her bedroom was nice and dark for sleeping, she turned *on* both of her lights.

For numbers 4 and 5, I am going to read sentences that contain words that are opposites. Listen for the opposite words, and write each pair on the numbered line on your paper.

4. The top of the picture is wider than the bottom.
5. The black print is easy to read on the white paper.

For number 6, I will read you a little story. On line number 6, make tally marks to count how many times you hear words that mean the same as *cut*.

It was time to prepare Thanksgiving dinner, and there was a job for everyone. Malcolm scrubbed and sliced potatoes. Tom chopped the onions and celery for the stuffing. Alice slit the fresh rolls and spread them with butter, and Bonnie carved the turkey.

(Teacher: For numbers 7 and 8, write the following on the board: 7. flower, flour; 8. road, rode.)

For numbers 7 and 8, look at the chalkboard. I will read a sentence using one of the words in each pair. Copy the word that I'm using on the numbered line on your paper.

7. My recipe calls for two cups of flour.
8. Ten children rode the bus to school.

Antonyms, Synonyms and Homonyms

(Teacher: For numbers 9 and 10, write the following on the board:
9. sail   sale   oar
10. stop   go   start)

Look at the words I've written on the board. Listen to my directions as you choose one word in each line to write on the numbered lines on your paper.

9. Write the word that is not part of a boat.
10. Write the word that means the opposite of the other two.

For numbers 11 and 12, think of your own answers to each direction I give you.

11. Write two homonyms that sound like *i*.
12. Write two synonyms for the word *sad*.

Opal Opposite

Skills:
Discerning mixed-up events with opposites

Materials:
Blank paper
Pencil

First draw a dotted line across the middle of your paper. This line should divide your paper into a top half and a bottom half. In the top of the top half, write your name. I'm going to tell you a story about a silly girl named Opal Opposite. Lots of times, Opal does just the opposite of what she should do. Every time you hear me tell something that Opal has backwards, make a tally mark in the top half of your paper. (Show students how to do this if necessary.) Listen carefully, because at the end of the story, I want you to draw a picture of one of the silly things Opal does.

Story:

"It's a beautiful day," thought Opal as she awoke. She smelled eggs and bacon cooking in the kitchen. "Mom must be fixing *supper*," said Opal.

"Wash your hands, dear," said Opal's mother as she walked into the kitchen. "Okay," replied Opal. She walked outside to get her hands clean in the *mud*!

After breakfast, Opal's mother asked her to get an old box of books out of the attic for her. Opal walked *downstairs* to get to the attic. When Opal found the right box, she noticed that the books were dusty and faded. Some of the pages had turned yellow. Others were ripped. "These books look brand *new*!" exclaimed Opal. The attic was chilly, and Opal's hands were cold. She decided to warm them by holding them under the *cold* water faucet.

Later, Opal's mother noticed the weather had turned warm and sunny. "Opal, this might be a good time to put on your new bathing suit and lay outside in the sun to start working on that suntan you've been wanting." "Great idea, Mom!" said Opal. She changed her clothes in their pool house and then went *inside* the house to get a tan.

At bedtime Opal remembered to wash her face and brush her *toes*! Then to make sure her bedroom was nice and dark for sleeping, she turned *on* both of her lights.

The End.

(Repeat story if necessary.)

Now count all the tally marks you've made. Write the number in the top half of your paper and circle it. In the bottom half of your paper, draw one of the silly "opposite" things that Opal did in the story.

Skills:
Distinguishing between antonyms and synonyms

Materials:
Just students

ANTONYMS, SYNONYMS AND HOMONYMS

Clap and Stomp

Use this page as a Warm-Up for Part 3.

In this activity, I will read you several pairs of words. If the words have the *same* meaning, stomp your feet. If the words have *opposite* meanings, clap your hands.

1. happy, glad
2. happy, sad
3. up, down
4. tiny, little
5. few, many
6. in, out
7. girl, gal
8. boy, lad
9. light, dark
10. bug, insect
11. off, on
12. job, chore

13. large, small
14. hard, soft
15. top, bottom
16. huge, big
17. ill, sick
18. quiet, peaceful
19. dirty, soiled
20. woman, lady
21. open, close
22. give, take
23. tear, rip
24. hot, cold

Skills:
Recognizing opposites

Materials:
Lined paper
Pencil

Hidden Opposites

Number your paper from 1 to 15. In this lesson, I am going to read sentences that contain words that are opposites. You are to listen carefully for the opposite words, and write them on the numbered lines on your paper. For example: If I read the sentence *The poor widow had three rich sons*, you would write the words *poor* and *rich* on your paper.

1. Please hang up the picture before you sit down.
   (Repeat each sentence once or twice.)

2. Alice is so short that everyone else seems tall.

3. Before you go to the store, please stop at the bank.

4. The lake will freeze in the winter and thaw in the spring.

5. This wet towel will get dry if we hang it in the sun.

6. The top of the picture frame is wider than the bottom.

7. We like the end of the book much better than the beginning.

8. My backpack is heavy as a rock, but my purse is light as a feather.

9. Let's put these hard candies in a dish next to the soft, chewy ones.

10. After I ate the sweet candy, my juice tasted sour.

11. The black print is easy to read on the white paper.

12. Why is it that summer vacation goes quickly, and the cold weather goes slowly?

In the next two sentences, try to find two pairs of opposites.

13. Most kids hate to lose and love to win.

14. Joe is always the first one to come to the party and the last one to leave.

15. Write your name on this line.

Skills:
Listening for synonyms

Materials:
Lined paper
Pencil

ANTONYMS, SYNONYMS AND HOMONYMS

Synonym Stories

Number your paper from 1 to 7. In this lesson I will read you seven little stories. In each one you need to listen for words that mean the same thing as the key word which I will tell you. You need to make tally marks to count how many times you hear words or phrases that have the same meaning or almost the same meaning as the key word.

1. In this first story, the key word is *marvelous*, as in "We had a marvelous time at the zoo." Every time you hear me say a word that means the same as *marvelous*, make a tally mark by number 1 on your paper.

   Ann's brother, Gary, planned a terrific party for her birthday. He baked a splendid chocolate cake, and he bought some excellent butter mints. Gary invited ten of Ann's friends, and he led the group in many wonderful games. After the party, Ann thanked Gary and said, "What a super party!"

2. In the second story, the key word is *cut*, as in "Don't cut your hands on the scissors."

   It was time to prepare Thanksgiving dinner, and there was a job for everyone. Malcolm scrubbed and sliced potatoes. Tom chopped the onions and celery for the stuffing. Alice slit the fresh rolls and spread them with butter, and Bonnie carved the turkey.

3. In the third story, the key word is *tall*, as in "My father is over six feet tall." We took a vacation last summer into the mountains. When we first saw them we couldn't believe how high they were! The towering trees looked like they were scraping the clouds. Birds were building nests in lofty branches. It was amazing!

4. In the fourth story, the key word is *wet*, as in "My beach towel is wet." Yesterday Patrick was playing at the park when he got caught in an unexpected rain shower. The rain came so hard that before Patrick could get home, his clothes were soaked. Even his shoes were soggy. His mother met him at the door and said, "Patrick, you're drenched! Let's get you into some dry clothes right away." As Patrick changed, he realized even his T-shirt and socks were damp. "Next time, I'll take an umbrella to keep me from getting doused," he thought.

Synonym Stories

5. In this fifth story, the key word is *rest*, as in "This afternoon, I just need to rest."
   It had been an exhausting vacation. The whole family was worn out. I'll lie down on the couch," said Mom. "I'll recline in my favorite chair," said Dad. "I'll relax in my room," Bryce said. "I'll unwind in my room," said Betsy. Luckily, there was a spot for everyone!

6. In the sixth story, the key word is *dirty*, as in "My hands are dirty from working in the garden."
   Bert was never crazy about doing laundry, but he knew someone had to do it, and since all his clothes were soiled, he thought he might as well get started. First he sorted the clothes. The grimy jeans went in one pile. The filthy work shirts and grubby socks went in another pile. His dingy undershirts went in a third pile. Bert looked at the mounds of unclean clothes and knew he'd be busy for awhile!

7. In the last story, the key word is *noise*, as in "The machine made a loud noise."
   When the elephant escaped from the zoo, there was uproar everywhere. "I don't know which is worse," the zookeeper exclaimed, "the racket of the banging, broken cage bars or the din of the screaming children!"

8. Write your name at the top of your page.

Optional Additional Activities:

A. Instruct students to listen carefully to some of the stories again, and then choose one to illustrate. They should include as many of the given details as possible.

B. Have students write their own "Synonym Stories." They may select their own sets of synonyms to use or select one from a list such as this one:

happy	big	sad	hard
rough	small	quiet	smart

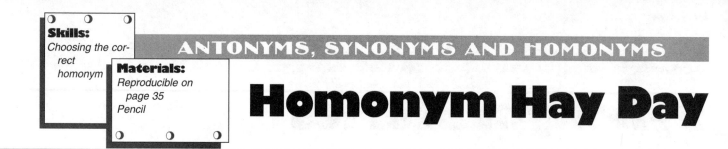

Skills:
Choosing the cor-
rect
homonym

Materials:
Reproducible on
page 35
Pencil

ANTONYMS, SYNONYMS AND HOMONYMS

Homonym Hay Day

Write your name in the top right corner of your paper. In this lesson, I will read sentences to you using some of the words listed on your paper. You need to listen carefully to the sentences to know which word (homonym) I am using. Then follow the directions I'll give you to mark your paper.

1. Look at the words by number 1. Which one is used in this sentence? The recipe calls for two cups of *flour*. Circle the correct *flour* with your pencil.

(Follow the same procedure with the following sentences.)

2. The wind *blew* the leaves off the roof.

3. The *doe* was caring for her new fawn.

4. We are having pie *for* dessert.

5. I cannot *hear* the radio.

6. Jasmyne *read* her favorite book five times.

7. We all *made* our beds this morning.

8. Ten children *rode* the bus to school.

9. My new *pair* of gloves is missing.

10. An octopus has *eight* arms.

11. The *knight* escaped from the dungeon and rescued the princess.

12. The teacher's final answer was "*no.*"

13. Bob will *sew* the button on his shirt.

For the last two lines, I will read you two sentences.

14. Susie will come with us, *too*. Circle the correct word.

    Let's write *to* the mayor. Underline the correct word.

15. I wonder if *they're* going home for Christmas. Circle the correct word.

    I set *their* gifts under the tree. Underline the correct word.

Homonym Hay Day

Reproducible for use with page 34.

1.	flower	flour	
2.	blew	blue	
3.	doe	dough	
4.	four	for	
5.	here	hear	
6.	red	read	
7.	made	maid	
8.	road	rode	
9.	pair	pear	
10.	ate	eight	
11.	night	knight	
12.	know	no	
13.	sew	so	
14.	to	too	two
15.	their	there	they're

Skills:
Identifying syn-
onyms,
antonyms
and
homonyms

Materials:
Reproducible on
page 37
Pencil

ANTONYMS, SYNONYMS AND HOMONYMS

Three's a Crowd

Write your name at the top of your page. You will notice that there are three words in each row. I am going to give directions that will tell you which word you should cross out in each line. When you've figured out my directions, just draw a line through the right word.

1. In row 1, cross out the word that sounds the same as the first word.

2. In row 2, cross out the word that means the opposite of the other two.

3. In row 3, cross out the word that is *not* an animal.

4. In row 4, cross out the word that is *not* a kind of coin.

5. In row 5, cross out the word that means the same as the first word.

6. In row 6, cross out the word that you cannot eat.

7. In row 7, cross out the word that means the opposite of the first word.

8. In row 8, cross out the word that is *not* part of a boat.

9. In row 9, there are two words that have almost the same meaning. Cross out the other word.

10. In row 10, there are two words that are opposites. Cross out the other word.

11. In row 11, cross out the word that sounds the same as the first word.

12. In row 12, cross out the word that is not a number word.

13. In row 13, cross out the word that means almost the same as the first word.

14. In row 14, cross out the word that cannot fly.

Three's a Crowd

Reproducible for use with page 36.

1.	write	right	left
2.	stop	go	start
3.	dear	deer	fawn
4.	cents	dime	sense
5.	mad	glad	angry
6.	meet	ham	meat
7.	new	old	knew
8.	sail	sale	oar
9.	quiet	peace	piece
10.	cell	sell	buy
11.	tail	tall	tale
12.	one	won	two
13.	sea	see	ocean
14.	bee	be	flea

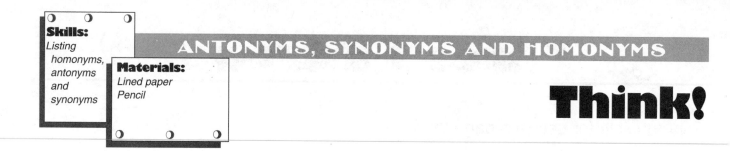

Skills:
Listing homonyms, antonyms and synonyms

Materials:
Lined paper
Pencil

ANTONYMS, SYNONYMS AND HOMONYMS

Think!

Number your paper from 1 to 15. Then listen carefully to my instructions. You will need to think of your own answers to each direction I give you.

1. Write an antonym for the word *soft.*

2. Write two synonyms for the word *happy.*

3. Write two homonyms that sound like *see.*

4. Write an antonym for the word *up.*

5. Write a synonym for the word *little.*

6. Write an antonym for the word *clean.*

7. Write two homonyms that sound like *I.*

8. Write a synonym for the word *kind.*

9. Write an antonym for the word *quiet.*

10. Write two homonyms that sound like *wood.*

11. Write an antonym for the word *dark.*

12. Write a synonym for the word *funny.*

13. Write an antonym for the word *top.*

14. Write two homonyms that sound like *by.*

15. Write two synonyms for the word *sad.*

16. Write your name at the bottom of your page.

Materials:
Lined paper
Pencil

Nouns, Verbs and Adjectives

Write your name in the top right corner of your page. Number from 1 to 10.

1. On line 1 write one of the nouns in this sentence: This is the house that Jack built.

2. On line 2 write a verb (or action word) that would complete this sentence:
The cow _____ .

For 3 and 4, I'll read three words. Listen carefully to decide which is not a noun.
Write the letter (A, B or C) of the word that is not a noun by the numbers on your
paper.

3.   A. drawer   B. thirsty   C. nose

4.   A. speak   B. hair   C. monkey

5. On line 5 write this sentence: The boy saw the fish.
Find two nouns and circle them. Find one verb (action word) and underline it.

6. On line 6 first write a noun that is a kind of animal. Next to it, write a verb that tells
something the animal did or does.

7. On line 7, use the two words in line 6 to write a simple sentence.
Use a capital letter at the beginning and a period at the end.

For 8 and 9, I will read sentences with the word *run*. Listen carefully to tell if *run* is
used as a noun or a verb. Write the word *noun* or *verb* to tell how it is used on the
numbered line on your paper.

8. Tim will *run* to home plate when the ball is hit.

9. Grandma has a *run* in her stocking.

For line 10, I will read a sentence. Listen carefully to learn how many words should
have capital letters. Each time you hear a word that should be capitalized, make a
tally mark on that line on your paper.

10. They all want to see the Pacific Ocean.

Noun, Verb, Adjective Warm-Ups

Noun Warm-Up

I am going to start a sentence. I want us to finish the sentence as many different ways as possible. We'll start with (name a student) and go as far around the room as possible. Listen carefully so you don't use a word that someone else has already used. (If desired, teacher could make a list on paper of all the nouns used and refer to them later as nouns, listing them on the board. *Not* listing them on the board during the activity requires students to be more attentive. Notice this lesson includes people, places and things.)

1. At the zoo I saw a _____.

2. At the bakery I could smell _____.

3. In my suitcase I packed a _____.

4. On my trip I went to _____.

5. Someday I'd like to meet _____.

6. One of my favorite people is my _____.

Verb Warm-Up

Go around the room as above. This time supply a name as given below, and ask the students to supply different verbs that begin with the same letter as the name. For example, the first sentence could be *Connie came* or *Connie counted* or *Connie camped.*

1. Connie _____.

2. Thomasina _____.

3. Sarah _____.

4. Bozo _____.

5. Ralph _____.

6. Delphi _____.

Adjective Warm-Up

Follow the same procedure as in the Noun Warm-Up, using these sentence starters:

1. Our class is very _____.

2. My pet cat is _____.

3. Our vacation was really _____.

4. The weather was _____.

5. The clown was very _____.

6. A factory is quite _____.

Literary Learning

Here's a fun and memorable way to introduce young students to nouns.*

1. First read the story, *The House That Jack Built* in its entirety.

2. Next, together with the students, think of a motion to each noun in the story. For instance, you may want to put your hands together in an upside-down *V* to represent the house. For Jack, the thumb and first finger of the right hand could be shaped into a *J*, etc.

3. After you've agreed on a motion, read the story again, slowly, with students listening carefully. Each time the students hear a noun, they should perform the appropriate motion.

4. At the end of the story, review the words that had motions, listing them on the board, if desired. Tell students these words are *nouns*, and encourage them to list more.

Optional Additional Activities:

• Have students illustrate some of the nouns from the story.
• Have students do "pattern" writing, substituting original nouns for those in the story.

*__Variation:__ Use a story such as *The Three Little Pigs* or *Goldilocks and the Three Bears* in a similar manner to introduce *verbs*.

Skills:
Copying nouns and adding verbs to make simple sentences

Materials:
Reproducible on page 43
Pencil

N O U N S , V E R B S A N D A D J E C T I V E S

Animal Action

Write your name at the top of your paper.

You can see a list of animal words on your paper. You'll also see some numbered lines with blanks in them. For each number, I'll start a sentence for you. You need to listen to the animal word I say, then find that word on the list and copy it into the first blank on the correct line on your paper. Then you need to finish each sentence by thinking of your own action word (or verb). For example, if I say "A fish blank," you might write, "A fish swims." Do your best on spelling. Try to use a different word to end each sentence.

1. In the first line in the first blank, write the word *tiger*. Your sentence will begin, *A tiger . . . .* Now finish this sentence with your own action word (or verb).

Follow the same procedure with the remaining sentences.

2. The duck . . .

3. A lion . . .

4. Some deer . . .

5. A mule . . .

6. The cow . . .

7. My turtle . . .

8. The horse . . .

9. Some sheep . . .

10. A rabbit . . .

42

Animal Action

Reproducible for use with page 42.

tiger	duck	cow
lion	deer	turtle
mule	sheep	horse
		rabbit

1. A _____ _____.

2. The _____ _____.

3. A _____ _____.

4. Some _____ _____.

5. A _____ _____.

6. The _____ _____.

7. My _____ _____.

8. The _____ _____.

9. Some _____ _____.

10. A _____ _____.

Skills:
Choosing which word is not a noun from a list of 3 words

Materials:
Lined paper
Pencil

NOUNS, VERBS AND ADJECTIVES

Not a Noun

Write your name in the top right corner of your paper. Number from 1 to 15. For each line on your paper, I will read three words. Listen carefully to decide which one of the three words is not a noun. Write the letter of the word (A, B or C) that is not a noun on the numbered line on your paper.

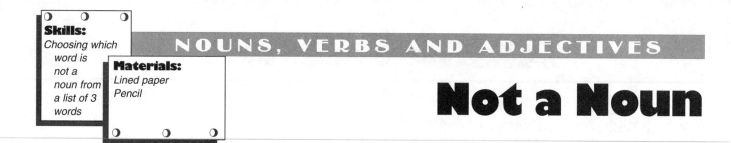

1. A. tomato   B. good   C. heart
2. A. acorn   B. tree   C. pollute
3. A. speak   B. monkey   C. hair
4. A. air   B. trash   C. laughing
5. A. drawer   B. thirsty   C. nose
6. A. wreath   B. boy   C. sing
7. A. think   B. sink   C. star
8. A. plum   B. net   C. wet
9. A. grow   B. card   C. Tom
10. A. Indiana   B. girl   C. purple
11. A. quick   B. earth   C. truck
12. A. pencil   B. hear   C. leg
13. A. computer   B. room   C. listen
14. A. difficult   B. playground C. chair
15. A. book   B. elbow   C. breathe

BOY! I'M a noun!

Descriptions

Skills:
Listing adjectives to describe concrete objects

Materials:
One or more collections of related items
Blank paper
Pencil

Bring in an assortment of kitchen gadgets, such as a potato peeler, an apple corer, a spatula, a gravy ladle, tongs, etc. Select one item to show to the class. Together on the board, for practice, make a list of adjectives that describe the item selected. For example, if the gadget selected was a potato peeler, the class might list these adjectives: sharp, hard, steel, useful, time-saver, etc.

Next show the remaining gadgets so everyone gets a good look at them. Divide the class into groups of three to four students. (Be sure you have more gadgets than groups.) Whisper to each group the name of the gadget they are to describe. Give each group a few minutes to write a list of adjectives which describe their assigned object. (If students are not able to write all the words, have them try to remember four to six words as a group.) Then have each group share their list while the other groups listen to guess which object is being described.

*In addition to kitchen gadgets, other sets of objects that could be used include:
    fruits
    vegetables
    work tools
    dollhouse furniture
    arts and crafts supplies
    sewing notions
    bottles and jars

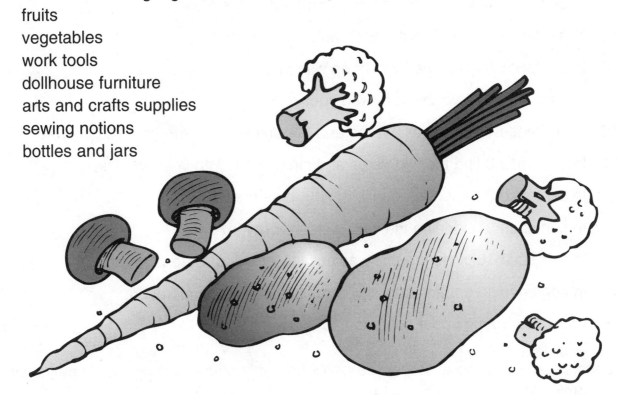

Skills:
Finding nouns, verbs and adjectives*

Materials:
Reproducible on page 47
Crayons: blue, red, green

NOUNS, VERBS AND ADJECTIVES

Colored Sentences

(Teacher: Read each sentence aloud with the class before reading the instructions for it.)

1. In sentence 1 circle the two nouns with your blue crayon.

2. In sentence 1 underline the verb with your red crayon.

3. In sentence 2 find a verb. Circle it in red.

4. In sentence 3 underline three adjectives with your green crayon.

5. In sentence 4 put a red box around the verb.

6. In sentence 4 circle the two nouns with your blue crayon.

7. In sentence 5 underline the verb with your red crayon.

8. In sentence 5 circle the two nouns with your blue crayon.

9. In sentence 6 circle the verb with your red crayon.

10. In sentence 7 find the two verbs and underline them with your red crayon.

11. In sentence 8 find the two verbs and circle them with your red crayon.

12. In sentence 9 circle the noun with your blue crayon.

13. In sentence 9 underline the verb with red crayon.

14. In sentence 10 circle the three adjectives with your green crayon.

15. In sentence 10 underline the two nouns with your blue crayon.

16. Write your name under sentence 10.

*Lesson can easily be altered so students find only nouns and verbs. Simply change (or omit) instructions #4 and #14.

Colored Sentences

Reproducible for use with page 46.

1. Ten yellow fish swam in a big pond.

2. A young boy dove into the pond.

3. He was very cold in the deep blue pond.

4. The boy saw the fish.

5. The boy grabbed the fish.

6. They swam away.

7. He walked out of the pond and dried himself.

8. The boy found his fishing pole and cast it into the pond.

9. The fish disappeared.

10. The sad little boy walked to his warm home.

Skills:
Adding correct parts of speech to simple sentences

Materials:
Lined paper
Pencil

NOUNS, VERBS AND ADJECTIVES

Sentence Building

Write your name in the top right corner of your paper. Number from 1 to 17.

1. On line 1 write a noun that is a kind of animal.

2. On line 2 write a verb that tells something the animal did or does.

3. On line 3 write the word *A* (with a capital *A*), then your noun, then your verb. Add a period at the end of the sentence.
Read it over to be sure it makes sense. If it doesn't, fix it.

4. Now think of an adjective that describes your animal. On line 4 rewrite your sentence on line 3 adding the adjective in front of the animal word.

5. On line 5 we will begin building a new sentence. On this line write a noun that represents a person. Don't use their name; instead use a word like *girl, cousin, people, man*, etc.

6. On line 6 write a verb that tells what your person might do.

7. On line 7 write the word *The* with a capital *T*, then your noun, then your verb. Again, add a period. Read the sentence over to be sure it makes sense. If it doesn't, try to fix it.

8. Now think of an adjective or describing word that tells about your person. On line 8 write your sentence from line 7, adding your describing word in front of your noun.

9. Now think of another adjective or describing word that fits your person. Rewrite your sentence in line 8, adding this new word after your first adjective.

10. On line 10 we'll begin another new sentence. This time think of a noun that names a place, such as a store, park, school, lunchroom, etc.

11. On line 11 write one of these verbs: is, was, will be.

12. On line 12 write this sentence starter: *The* (with a capital *T*), your noun and your verb.

Sentence Building

13. Now think of an adjective or describing word that tells about your place. On line 13 rewrite the sentence starter from line 12, this time adding the adjective and a period. Check your sentence over to be sure it makes sense. If it doesn't, try to fix it.

14. On line 14 we'll start a new sentence. On line 14 write any noun that names an object.

15. On line 15 write any action word or action verb of your choice.

16. On line 16 write any adjective of your choice.

17. On line 17 write these sentences, leaving large blanks where I tell you: Yesterday I saw a (blank). It could (blank), and it was very (blank).

18. Now look at the word you wrote on line 14. Add it to the first blank on line 17. Look at the word you wrote on line 15. Write it in the second blank on line 17. Find the word you wrote on line 16. Write it in the last blank on line 17.

Does your last sentence make sense? Is it silly?
Select one of your new sentences, from line 4, 9, 13 or 17. Draw a picture of it on the back of your paper.

(Teacher: You may want to allow time for students to share their finished sentences with the rest of the class. You may also want to save sentences for use in future lessons when reviewing these parts of speech. Students love to see their own sentences used on the board as examples!)

Skills:
Determining if a
word is
used as a
noun or a
verb with-
in a sen-
tence

Noun or Verb?

Number your paper from 1 to 20. Write your name in the top left corner of your page. In this lesson I will ask you to listen to how a particular word is being used in a sentence. For example, listen to the word *ring* in these two sentences:

The circus master pointed to the elephants in the first *ring*.

Tommy will *ring* the bell for recess.

In the first sentence the word *ring* is used as a *noun*. It is a thing, or a place where the elephants are performing. In the second sentence, *ring* is used as a *verb,* or action word, to tell what Tommy is doing with the bell.

Now I will read several sentences. Write the word *noun* or *verb* on each line on your paper to tell how the special word in each sentence is being used. Sometimes I will use the same word in different ways, and sometimes I will use it the same way twice, so listen carefully!

1. run   Tim will *run* to home plate when the ball is hit.

2. run   Grandma has a *run* in her stocking.

3. bank   The river *bank* is covered with moss.

4. bank   I will keep my money in the *bank*.

5. drive   Could you *drive* me to the store, please?

6. drive   Sue had her *drive* covered with blacktop.

7. ball   Jan hit the *ball* over the fence.

8. ball   Cinderella met the prince at the *ball*.

Noun or Verb?

9. water   Please *water* the flowers in the front yard.

10. water   That drink of *water* really tasted good!

11. play   Albert has the part of George Washington in the school *play*.

12. play   Violet will *play* soccer this Saturday.

13. sink   That heavy toy will *sink* in the pond.

14. sink   Martha scrubbed the kitchen *sink*.

15. note   My mom wrote a *note* to the teacher.

16. note   The doctor will *note* your illness in the records.

17. bat   The *bat* flew into the birdhouse.

18. bat   She will *bat* the ball out of the park.

19. rest   Please *rest* your feet on this footstool.

20. rest   After a long day, it's nice to *rest* on the sofa.

Skills:
Listening for proper nouns

Materials:
Lined paper
Pencil

NOUNS, VERBS AND ADJECTIVES

Capital Sentences

(Before the lesson review capitalization rules if necessary.)
Number your paper from 1 to 13. For each number, I will read a sentence. Listen carefully to learn how many words should be capitalized in each sentence. Each time you hear a word that should be capitalized, make a tally mark on that line on your paper. Remember, the first word is always capitalized!

1. On Saturday, Joshua and Elizabeth will travel to Texas.

2. It will be their first time to travel in an airplane.

3. They hope they can see the Mississippi River from the plane.

4. They will land in Austin.

5. Their dad, Dr. Smith, will look at a new hospital.

6. If he likes it, the family will move to Texas in May.

7. The children would like to live on Maple Street right next to a park.

8. Mrs. Smith wants to live near the Austin Public Library.

9. Another family, the Miltons, are hoping to travel to California.

10. They will fly on American Airlines.

11. Mrs. Milton wants to see the mountains.

12. They all want to see the Pacific Ocean.

13. Write your name on this line.

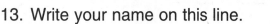

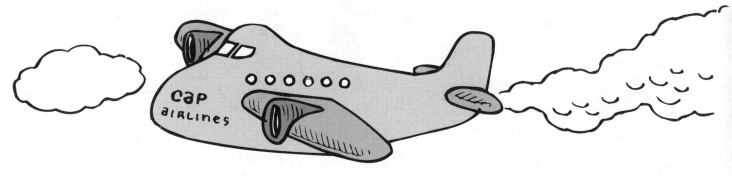

Materials:
Lined paper
Pencil

Rhymes and Poetry

Number your paper from 1 to 13. Be sure to leave two lines for number 10. Write your name in the top right corner of your page.

For numbers 1 and 2, I will read a pair of words. If the words rhyme, write *yes* on your paper, If the words do not rhyme, write *no* on your paper.

1. fold   cold

2. stake   leak

For numbers 3 and 4, I will read a list of words. Your job is to listen to how many words rhyme with the first word that I say. Count the number of rhyming words in each list, and write that number on the correct line on your paper.

3. First word: pig   Other words: big, word, gig, dig, on

4. First word: bib   Other words: crib, drop, tube, rib, lot

(Teacher: For 5-7, write these rows of words on the board:

   A.   bird   hen   when

   B.   bus   done   come)

Now look at the words on the board. For 5, 6 and 7, you will write one of these words by the correct number on your paper.

5. Write the animal word from line A that rhymes with *then*.

6. Write the word from line B that rhymes with *sum*.

7. Write the word from line B that rhymes with *run*.

For numbers 8 and 9, I will read a short poem where each word begins with a different letter of the alphabet, in order. The poem can start at any letter and use the next few letters in order. On your paper, write just the beginning letters of the words I say.

8. Betsy
   Can
   Do
   Everything!

9. Ralph
   Stole
   Tommy's
   Umbrella.

Rhymes and Poetry

10. For number 10, I will read the beginning of a short poem. You need to write down every word that I read and then finish the poem. The rhyme starter is *My old cat/Has a* _____. Write the words *My old cat* on the first line. Write the words *Has a* on the second line. Finish the second line with a word that rhymes with the last word of the first line.

For 11 and 12, I will read a haiku. Then I will give you three choices of what the poem was about. Write the letter of the correct choice (A, B or C) on the line on your paper.*

11. Layers of color
    Curving across sunny clouds
    After the rain ends.
    A. thunderstorm   B. rainbow   C. snowstorm

12. Growing, giving life
    To blossoms, fruits and shade
    Bark, branches and leaves.
    A. river   B. grass   C. tree

13. For number 13, I will read a limerick, leaving out the last word.
    Then I will give you three choices of words to complete the poem. Write the letter of your choice (A, B or C) on the line on your paper.*
    A cow from the city of Dover
    Just loved to graze on sweet clover.
    When his friends asked him out
    He'd cry and he'd shout,
    "I'm EATING. I cannot come _____.
    A. there   B. over   C. today

*For older students, alternate directions could be given, asking the students to supply an appropriate word without listing three choices. See corresponding lessons.

Up and Down

Skills:
Distinguishing rhyming and non-rhyming words

Materials:
Just students

Use this page as a Warm-Up for Part 6.

For this activity, I am going to say several pairs of words. If both words in the pair *do* rhyme, stand up. If the words *do not* rhyme, sit down.

1. fun, run
2. rule, tool
3. fold, cold
4. do, toe
5. house, sound
6. book, look
7. stake, leak
8. bill, built

9. men, then
10. feet, meant
11. poke, hole
12. yes, mess
13. cow, now
14. hold, melt
15. hush, rush
16. once, mug

17. boot, suit
18. mince, mint
19. fat, chart
20. quit, slit
21. text, next
22. busy, silly
23. shelf, help
24. zipper, dipper

Skills:
Listening for rhyming words

Materials:
Lined paper
Pencil

Rows of Rhymes

Write your name in the top right corner of your page. Number the lines on your paper from 1 to 12. For each number, I am going to read a row of words. Your job is to listen to how many words rhyme with the first word I say. Count the number of rhyming words in each row, and write that number on the line on your paper.
(Teacher: Do the first one together.)

1. In line 1 the first word is *sat.* Listen to how many of these other five words rhyme with *sat: cat, bat, still, that, rat.* (Repeat first word and following words.) Write the number of rhyming words by the number 1 on your paper. Did you write four? There were four rhyming words: *cat, bat, that* and *rat.* We'll do the rest this same way.

2. First word: pig   Other words: big, word, gig, dig, on

3. First word: call   Other words: shawl, pole, haul, ball, fall

4. First word: bath   Other words: joy, path, math, band, hat

5. First word: dust   Other words: must, sleigh, key, just, rust

6. First word: sing   Other words: king, ding, swing, bring, sling

7. First word: hash   Other words: sash, pen, cash, dash, bash

8. First word: wet   Other words: bet, set, bed, cot, let

9. First word: stop   Other words: mop, sop, cop, pop, hop

10. First word: when   Other words: Ben, Ken, pen, men, pan

11. First word: chair   Other words: bear, share, barn, air, pair

12. First word: bib   Other words: crib, drop, tube, rib, lot

JOY MATH HAT PATH BAND

Rhyme Reasoning 1

Skills:
Finding words that rhyme and fit other clues

Materials:
Reproducible on page 58
Pencil

Write your name in the top right corner of your page.

1. Circle the animal word in line 1 that rhymes with *then*.

2. Circle the color word in line 2 that rhymes with *bread*.

3. Circle the longest word in line 3 that rhymes with *day*.

4. Circle the shortest word in line 4 that rhymes with *two*.

5. Circle the only word in line 5 that rhymes with *run*.

6. Circle the word in line 6 that rhymes with *train* and is a part of the body.

7. Circle the word in line 7 that rhymes with *hose* and names a flower.

8. Circle the word in line 8 that does *not* rhyme with *some*.

9. Circle the word in line 9 that rhymes with *cut* and means the opposite of *open*.

10. Circle all the words in line 10 that rhyme with *meat*.

11. Circle the word in line 11 that rhymes with *green* and names something you eat.

12. Circle the word in line 12 that does *not* rhyme with *money*.

Rhyme Reasoning

Reproducible for use with pages 57 and 59.

1.	bird	hen	when
2.	red	blue	said
3.	play	say	sleigh
4.	boo	do	clue
5.	bus	done	come
6.	crane	brain	heart
7.	rose	toes	tulip
8.	numb	hum	jump
9.	close	shut	nut
10.	seat	greet	feet
11.	bean	seen	plum
12.	funny	shiny	honey

Rhyme Reasoning 2

Skills:
Finding words that rhyme and fit other clues

Materials:
Reproducible on page 58
Pencil

This activity may be done on the same reproducible as "Rhyme Reasoning 1," if desired.

Write your name in the top right corner of your page.

1. Underline the word in line 5 that rhymes with *sum*.

2. Underline the word in line 8 that rhymes with *come* and is a musical sound you make with your mouth.

3. Underline the only word in line 2 that does *not* rhyme with *head*.

4. Underline the word in line 12 that rhymes with *bunny* and is something sweet to eat.

5. Underline the word in line 7 that rhymes with *close* and is part of the body.

6. Underline the longest word in line 10 that rhymes with *beat*.

7. In line 1 underline the word that does *not* rhyme with *men*.

8. In line 4 underline the word that rhymes with *zoo* and means "a hint."

9. In line 11 underline the word that does *not* rhyme with *lean*.

10. In line 9 underline the word that rhymes with *hut* and is something you eat.

11. In line 6 underline the word that rhymes with *lane* and names a large piece of equipment.

12. In line 3 underline the word that rhymes with *clay* and is something you do with toys.

Skills:
Listening for beginning sounds

Materials:
Lined paper
Pencil

ABC–Listen!

ABC poetry is fun! Here are two examples:
(Teacher: Put these on the board. You may also want to have the entire alphabet written out within easy view of the students.)

Always   **D**on't
Bring   **E**at
Cookies   **F**udge
                    Greedily!

Notice that the first letter in each line is a different letter of the alphabet, in order. The first poem uses the first three letters of the alphabet, but you can start anywhere in the alphabet and use the next few letters in order. Let's try to think of our own for the letters *L, M* and *N* just to make sure you have the idea. (Brainstorm together. Possible outcome: Lisa Makes Noodles.)

Now I want you to number your paper from 1 to 11. Write your name by the number 1. Next, I will read you 10 little ABC poems. I want you to listen to the beginning sounds of the words I am saying and figure out which part of the alphabet is used for each poem. Then write those letters of the alphabet on the line on your paper. For example, if I read the "fudge" poem to you that's on the board, you would write down "D E F G." Let's begin.

2. Jumping
    Kangaroos
    Like
    Milk.

3. Betsy
    Can
    Do
    Everything!

4. Ralph
    Stole
    Tommy's
    Umbrella.

5. Get
    Help
    In
    June.

6. Obey
    Parents
    Quickly.

7. Carlos
    Digs
    Early
    For
    Grubs.

8. Seven
    Tigers
    Unfolded
    Violet's
    Wallet.

9. Frank
    Gave
    Harriet
    Indian
    Jewels.

10. Let
    Mindy
    Name
    Our
    Pet.

11. Nora
    Ordered
    Purple
    Quilts.

Dictated Rhymes

Skills:
Writing from dictation*
Completing rhymes

Materials:
Lined paper
Pencil

Write your name at the top of your paper. Number from 1 to 10, leaving two lines for each number. In this lesson, I will read the beginning of a little rhyme. I want you to write the words that I read. Where I leave a blank, I want you to think of your own word that rhymes and makes sense. You should know how to spell most of the words that you hear, but if you don't, just do your best. Let's do the first one together so you can be sure how to do it.

Here's the first rhyme starter: *Here I see/A little _____*. Now write the first three words, *Here I see* on the first line. Right under that, write the rest of the rhyme, *A little ___* and think of your own word that goes in the blank. What are some good choices of words you could use to finish this rhyme? (Possible choices include *bee* and *key*.) Now let's do the rest. These poems will all have two lines, and I'll always tell you where to start the second line. The word that you think of needs to rhyme with the last word in the first line, just like in the poem we did together.

Follow the same procedure with these:

2. My old cat

   Has a _____.

3. On this day

   I want to _____.

4. I like to eat

   A little _____.

5. In the den

   I saw a _____.

6. In the road

   I found a _____.

7. How does it feel

   To be a _____?

8. By and by

   I'll get a _____.

9. Put the fox

   In a _____.

10. I will plan

    To find a _____.

*These couplets can also be used orally for younger students. Try to see how many sensible rhyming solutions the class can find.

Also, this lesson will be too long for some students when doing dictation. Use just a few at a time if desired.

Skills:
Finding the topic
of a
haiku

Materials:
Lined paper
Pencil

Haiku

The Japanese people invented a beautiful kind of poetry called haiku. These are very short poems, and they do not have rhyming words. They have three lines, usually with five syllables in the first line, seven syllables in the second line and five syllables in the last line. Haiku poetry usually describes something found in nature. Here is an example of a haiku:

> Layers of color
> Curving across sunny clouds
> After the rain ends.

What do you think this haiku is describing? That's right, it's a rainbow. (Discuss the clues in the poem with the class if necessary.)

Write your name at the top of your paper. Now I want you to number your paper from 1 to 10. I am going to read you 10 different haiku poems, and I want you to listen closely so you can tell what each one is about.

(Teacher: Use one of these sets of instructions, depending on the level of students:

A. At the end of each haiku, I will give you three choices. Write the letter of the answer, *A, B* or *C*, that tells what that haiku was about. OR

B. At the end of each haiku, write the name of the object you think the haiku is describing.)

1. Blowing, drifting snow   A. tornado   B. blizzard   C. earthquake
   Piling high above our boots
   Walking is hard.

2. A zoo animal   A. zebra   B. tiger   C. bear
   Black and white horse-like body
   Interesting stripes.

3. Growing, giving life   A. river   B. grass   C. tree
   To blossoms, fruits and shades
   Bark, branches and leaves.

Haiku

4. Big hot ball of fire
   Grows our food and keeps us warm
   Bright light in the sky.

   A. match   B. sun   C. moon

5. Tumbling and roaring
   Bubbling, moving so quickly
   Falling down wet–SPLASH!

   A. mountain   B. river   C. waterfall

6. Friendly, welcome pet
   Comes in all shapes and sizes
   He is man's best friend.

   A. dog   B. spider   C. skunk

7. Leaves changing color
   Squirrels preparing for winter
   Season of harvest.

   A. summer   B. fall   C. winter

8. Sunny, hot and dry
   Cactus, lizards, lots of sand
   No break from the heat.

   A. desert   B. ocean   C. playground

9. Beautiful flower
   That has a very sweet smell
   And a thorny stem.

   A. tulip   B. dandelion   C. rose

10. Fuzzy, wuzzy worm
    Soon you will spin a cocoon
    Then you will be changed.

    A. snake   B. caterpillar   C. butterfly

Optional Additional Activities:

*Illustrate one or more of the haiku above.
*Write original haiku for these or other topics: mountain, ocean, cat, river, apple, spring, mushroom, volcano, kangaroo, whale, etc.

All haiku written by Ann Richmond Fisher.

Skills:
Finishing limericks

Materials:
Paper
Pencil

Limerick Lessons

(Teacher: The limericks that follow can be used in three different ways:
1. Omit the last word. Give students three choices of possible last words. Instruct them to write their choice—A, B or C—on their paper. [These are the instructions that follow since they are the easiest for young students.]
2. Omit the last word and ask students to supply it without giving them choices.
3. Omit the last line and ask students to compose the entire line.)

Today's lesson is about limericks. Limericks are funny rhyming poems like this one. (Write sample limerick on board.) Can you find the rhyme patterns? That's right—the first, second and fifth lines all rhyme. The third and fourth lines rhyme with each other and are shorter than the other ones. (Read more limericks, if desired, from other resources.)

Sample limerick: In a little village called Locko
                         There lived a young boy named Paco.
                         He liked meat with cheese
                         And some lettuce, please.
                         For his favorite food was a taco.

Number your paper from 1 to 10. I will read you a limerick, leaving out the last word. Then I will read three possible words to complete the poem. Figure out which word fits the rhyme pattern and makes sense. Write the letter of that answer (A, B or C) on the numbered line on your paper. Write your name at the top of your paper.

1. A cow from the city of Dover
   Just loved to graze on sweet clover.
   When his friends asked him out
   He'd cry and he'd shout,
   "I'm EATING! I cannot come _____."

   A. there   B. over   C. today

2. An eager young chef named Freddy
   Wanted to cook some spaghetti.
   He made a mistake–
   What an unlucky break!
   The noodles turned out like _____.

   A. glitter   B. ready   C. confetti

Limerick Lessons

3. There was a man known as a crook
   Who wanted to learn how to cook.
   He went out and stole
   A spoon and a bowl
   Then baked a cake someone else __!

   A. took   B. shook   C. grabbed

4. A clever, white furry bunny
   Was working to earn lots of money.
   His idea worked well
   He decided to sell
   To a bear a pot full of _____.

   A. sunny   B. fish   C. honey

5. A girl who always walked on the ceiling
   Was often asked, "How are you feeling?"
   "Just fine," she'd reply,
   "But, oh, by the by,
   The paint on the ceiling is _____."

   A. peeling   B. heeling   C. cracked

6. A silly, fun clown whose name was Will
   Mistakenly swallowed a laughing pill.
   He choked and he chuckled
   Till his belt came unbuckled
   And Clown Will is probably laughing __.

   A. today   B. still   C. hill

7. A tall man who was very proud
   Always bragged in a voice that was loud.
   "I'm so tall and thin
   That to see my grin
   You'll all have to climb on a _____!"

   A. cloud   B. plowed   C. ladder

8. An old goat who was always sick
   Was seen by a vet named Rick.
   "I know what's wrong,
   And it won't take long.
   From your stomach I'll take out that __!

   A. kick   B. brick   C. garbage

9. There was a young boy who hated
     to brush
   Because he was in too much of a rush.
   When his teeth rotted out
   He just said with a pout,
   "Now meals will be faster.
     I'll just eat _____."

   A. blush   B. meat   C. mush

10. A dog who didn't know how to bark
    Thought he could learn how at the
      park.
    He watched and he heard
    How to bark from a bird
    Then the dog sounded just like a __.

    A. spark   B. lark   C. robin

All limericks written by Ann Richmond Fisher.

Listening Comprehension

1. Look at the pictures in line A. Hans Christian Andersen was a famous writer. When he was a little boy, his family was very poor. His father made shoes, and his mother washed clothes for other people. Find the picture of the lady washing clothes. Shade the lady's shirt with your pencil.

2. One of the fairy tales Hans wrote was *The Princess and the Pea*. Find the picture of the princess sleeping on the stack of mattresses. Look for the pea in her bed. Shade it in with your pencil.

3. Look at the clowns in line B. One of them is named Clyde. I will read you two clues so you can find out which one is Clyde. When you've found Clyde, put a *C* on his hat. Clues: a. Clyde is not wearing stripes. b. Clyde has curly hair. Remember to put a *C* on Clyde's hat.

4. One of the clowns is my brother. Any of the three, including Clyde, might be my brother. Listen again to two clues to help you. Clues: a. My brother has a round nose. b. My brother doesn't wear polka dots. Put a *B* under my brother.

5. Listen to this little story about Monster Monkey. Then write answers to the questions in the blanks by letters *C* and *D*. **Story:** Once there was a little monkey who was very brave. He liked to chase big ferocious animals. He chased elephants, lions and tigers. He even chased porcupines; he wasn't scared of their pricklers! Because this little monkey was so brave, he was named Monster Monkey. **Questions:** C. Why was this animal named Monster? Write *W* if it was because he was wimpy. Write *S* if it was because he was shy. Write *B* if it was because he was brave. D. What kind of animal was Monster? Write *E* for elephant, *M* for monkey or *C* for cheetah.

6. On line E, write the word *pig*. Listen to these directions to change it into something else.

7. On line F, copy the letters from line E, but change the *G* to a *W*.

8. Now copy the letters from line F to line G, adding an *O* between the first and second letters. You should have four letters.

9. Now change the first letter to a *C*, and copy the letters onto line H. You still have four letters.

10. Now write the letters again on line I, removing the third letter. Your pig has now become a different animal!

11. Write your name in box J.

Listening Comprehension

Reproducible for use with page 66.

A.

B.

C. _____ D. _____

E. _____

F. _____

G. _____

H. _____

J.

I. _____

Skills:
Listening to and following directions

Materials:
Just students

Teacher, May I?

Use this page as a Warm-Up for Part 6.

As a warm-up to simple listening comprehension, play this variation of an old game.

The teacher has the entire class stand against a wall (either in the classroom, the gym or the hallway). The teacher calls out various directions. If the instruction pertains to a student, he must ask, "Teacher, may I?" The teacher responds either, "Yes, you may," or "No, you may not." If given permission, the student then proceeds to carry out the instruction. The goal is to be the first child to reach the opposite wall or some other specific location in the room. The children need to listen to learn if the instruction is for them and what they are to do. While directions will vary according to students in the group, here some samples.

    a. Everyone with blue eyes, take 2 little steps forward.
    b. All boys wearing red, take 5 big steps forward.
    c. Everyone with blond hair and brown eyes, take 3 little steps backward.
    d. All girls with an *R* in their first name, take 1 big step forward.
    e. Everyone whose last name begins with a consonant, take 4 big steps forward.
    f. Everyone who rides a bus to school, take 2 little steps backward.
And so on.

Skills:
Acting out stories

Materials:
Any copy of some of Aseop's fables

Fabled Skits

Tell students they will have an opportunity to act out some very interesting animal stories. Arrange them in groups of three to four students. Read several Aesop's Fables to the entire class. (Choose ones with few characters and enough action for your students to act out. *The Tortoise and the Hare* is a good example.) Then ask each group to select one to perform. As a group, they need to assign parts (sometimes including a narrator), decide on and practice lines, decide where to stand, etc. After the groups have made such decisions, read each fable again, giving students another opportunity to listen for details. Then give groups another work session. Finally, allow groups to perform!

Hans Christian Andersen

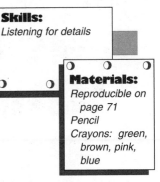

Skills:
Listening for details

Materials:
Reproducible on page 71
Pencil
Crayons: green, brown, pink, blue

Look at the six pictures on your paper. I'm going to tell you about a famous writer, and during different parts of the story I'll ask you to find a picture that tells something about his life. I will ask you to follow some instructions for that picture. Listen carefully so you know what to do.

Story:

Hans Christian Andersen lived in the 1800s. He was born in Denmark. His family was very poor, and he was a thin, homely boy. Hans' father was a cobbler. That means he made and repaired shoes. Find the picture on your page that shows shoes. Color one shoe brown. Color the other one blue.

Hans' mother also worked to earn money for the family. Her job was to wash clothes for other people. Find the picture of the lady washing clothes. Color the lady's shirt green.

As Hans was growing up, he was a dreamer. He liked to play with puppets. Perhaps that is when he first started making up stories. Neighborhood children would laugh at him, and some adults said he was a fool. But that didn't stop Hans from working hard at what he enjoyed.

When Hans was just 14, he left home with only a little money from his piggy bank. He went to a larger city called Copenhagen, where he tried very hard to become an actor, singer or dancer. He almost starved. Find the picture on your paper of the dancer. Write your name in this box.

Then a theater director became a good friend and helped Hans go back to school to finish his education. School was hard for Hans because he was older than the other students. The others would pick on him and tease him. He was a shy, lonely young man.

Soon after he attended college, Hans Christian Andersen began to write stories that were printed for others to read. When he was 30, his first fairy tales were published. One of his first fairy tales was *The Princess and the Pea*. Do you know that story? On your page, find the picture of the princess sleeping on the stack of mattresses. Look for the pea in her bed, and when you've found it, color it green.

Hans Christian Andersen

Another famous story written by Mr. Andersen is *The Ugly Duckling*. Have you heard the story? It is the story of an ugly baby duck that grows up to be a beautiful swan. Many people have said that story tells the story of Hans Christian Andersen, the shy, poor, lonely boy who grew up to be a famous, well-loved author. Find the picture on your page of the duckling and the swan. Color the duckling brown.

Another one of his famous stories is *The Little Mermaid*. The people of Copenhagen, Denmark, made a statue of the mermaid who fell in love in their harbor to honor Hans Christian Andersen. Find the picture of the mermaid on your paper. Color her clothes pink. Color the water by her blue.

In all, Hans Christian Andersen wrote 168 fairy tales plus poetry, novels, plays and other articles and books. His writings are now translated into more than 100 languages. Everyone who has ever enjoyed one of Mr. Andersen's stories is happy that Hans didn't let hard times hold him back from what he did best.

Additional Activities:

*Please read some of Andersen's tales to your class as a rewarding follow-up to this lesson. In addition to the tales mentioned in the story, a few of his fairy tales are listed here:

    The Emperor's New Clothes
    The Snow Queen
    The Red Shoes
    The Tinderbox
    The Little Match Girl
    The Constant Tin Soldier

*Discuss and/or read about other famous people who overcame difficult circumstances to become famous and productive adults. Two such examples are Helen Keller and Abraham Lincoln.

Hans Christian Andersen

Reproducible for use with pages 69 and 70.

Skills:
Listening for details

Materials:
Reproducible on
  page 73
Pencil
Crayons: blue, red, green

LISTENING COMPREHENSION

Snowmen

(Teacher: In this lesson, students will select the one correct choice out of four possibilities, using simple clues. To help them keep track of clues, show them how to write a light *X* in boxes as they are eliminated. You could suggest that they *X* a different corner of the box for each set of clues.)

1. Look at your page of four snowmen. Did you know that one of these snowmen is yours? Listen closely to some clues to find out which one is yours.
   a. Your snowman has three "fingers" on each hand.
   b. Your snowman has a carrot nose.
   c. Your snowman has both a scarf and a hat.
   By now you should know which snowman is yours. Write your name under your snowman with your blue crayon, and color his scarf blue.

2. Did you know that your teacher built one of these snowmen? Your teacher may have built yours or any of the others. Here are the clues to learn which one your teacher built.
   a. Of course, your teacher put a big, happy smile on the snowman.
   b. Your teacher put a scarf on the snowman.
   c. Your teacher put more than three buttons on the snowman.
   Now you should know which snowman your teacher built. Color the scarf on your teacher's snowman red.

3. Next we're going to find out which snowman the mayor built.
   a. Your mayor's snowman has a carrot nose.
   b. Your mayor used either a hat or a scarf but not both.
   When you've found the mayor's snowman, underline it with your green crayon.

4. One of these snowmen won first prize in a neighborhood snowman contest. It could be yours, your teacher's, the mayor's or the fourth snowman. Here are the clues to find it.
   a. The winning snowman had more than two buttons.
   b. The winning snowman had both a scarf and a hat.
   c. The winning snowman's scarf was *not* red.
   Have you found the winner? Draw a blue star in the top part of the box of the winning snowman.

Snowmen

Reproducible for use with page 72.

Skills:
Listening for sequence and details

Materials:
Lined paper
Pencil

LISTENING COMPREHENSION

Monster Monkey

Write your name in the top left corner of your paper. Then number the lines on your paper from 1 to 10. I'm going to read a story called "Monster Monkey." At the end of the story, I will ask you several questions. Listen carefully so you will know the answers.

Story:
Once there was a little monkey who was very brave. He liked to chase big ferocious animals. He chased elephants, lions and tigers. He even chased porcupines; he wasn't scared of their pricklers! Because this little monkey was so brave, he was named Monster Monkey.

One hot morning, Monster Monkey woke up and got out of his bed made of leaves and branches. As always, Monster ate a big breakfast of ripe, sweet bananas. "Yum, yum," he said. Then he jumped away from the table and hit his head on a branch in his tree house. Since the jungle is too hot for ice packs, Monster found some cool leaves to hold on his hurting head. After his head cooled, Monster carefully climbed down out of the tree.

Monster then went to find some animals to chase. He only wanted to chase the ferocious ones. First he met Grandpa Ape. "I don't want to chase Grandpa," thought Monster. "He's not ferocious." Next he met Lazy Lyza Lizard. "She won't be much fun to chase. She moves too slowly," thought Monster. Finally he came upon Evan Elephant. "I'll chase him—he's ferocious!" And Monster spent the rest of the morning chasing Evan Elephant. Evan was relieved when Monster finally said, "Munchtime!"

Monster ran home and while he was climbing up to his tree house, he bumped his head again! Poor Monster! He found some more cool leaves to rub on his second "ouchy." When he felt better he ate a lunch of coconut milk and mangoes. He climbed back down his tree house and ran out to look for someone else to chase.

This time he found Charlie Cheetah. He chased Charlie until supper time. This time Monster ate kiwi and coconut milk. Then Monster was so tired that he went straight to bed.

The End.

(Repeat story if necessary.)

Monster Monkey

1. What kind of animal was Monster? Write *E* for elephant; write *M* for monkey; or write *C* for cheetah.

2. Why was this animal named Monster? Write *W* if it was because he was wimpy. Write *S* if it was because he was shy. Write *B* if it was because he was brave.

3. What did Monster eat for breakfast? Write *B* for bananas, *K* for kiwi or *E* for eggs.

4. What did Monster do right after breakfast? Write *N* if he took a nap. Write *J* if he jumped from the table and bumped his head. Write *L* if he ate leaves.

5. When Monster went out the first time to find an animal to chase, whom did he first meet? Write *E* for Evan Elephant; write *C* for his cousin; write *G* for Grandpa Ape.

6. How many times did Monster bump his head? Write the number *1, 2* or *3*.

7. What did Monster put on his head when it hurt? Write *I* for ice packs; write *L* for leaves; write *W* for water.

8. Where did Monster live? Write *T* for tree house; write *I* for igloo; write M for mountain.

9. Who did Monster chase after lunch? Write *L* for Lazy Lyza Lizard; write *F* for his father; write *C* for Charlie Cheetah.

10. What did Monster do right after supper? Write *C* for chase another animal; write *B* for go to bed; write *S* for sit down.

Skills: Understanding and following directions

Materials: Lined paper Pencil

Puppy Love

In this lesson, you are going to change a puppy into another animal. Listen carefully to my directions and you will be able to find out what the new animal is. First number your paper from 1 to 11. Each time I give an instruction, write the new set of letters on the next numbered line.

1. On line 1 write the word PUPPY. It is spelled P-U-P-P-Y.

2. Rewrite the letters on line 2, adding the letter *O* between the third and fourth letters. You should have six letters to write on line 2.

3. Now write the letters on line 3 removing the first letter. You should have five letters.

4. Rewrite the letters on line 4, adding a *D* between the second and third letters.

5. Write the letters again, this time on line 5. As you do this, remove the sixth letter. You should have five letters.

6. Now add a *G* at the beginning of the letters as you rewrite all the letters on line 6.

7. Now write the letters on line 7, removing the second letter.

8. Now write all but the last letter on line 8. You should have four letters.

9. Remove the second letter. Write the letters you still have on line 9.

10. Now move the first letter to the end of the other letters, and write all the letters on line 10. What has your puppy become? If you've followed all the directions, you'll know.

11. Finally, write your name on line 11.

Answer Key

Pre/Posttest, Part 1, page 2

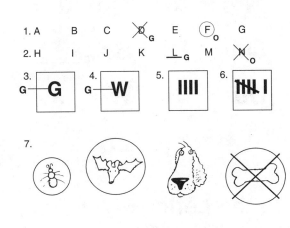

1. A B C ~~D~~ E Ⓕ G
2. H I J K L̲ G M ~~N~~ O

3. G—| G | 4. G—| W | 5. | IIII | 6. | ℟𝖧𝖫 I |

7.

8. st _e_ p   m _o_ p   t _a_ n

9. _2_

Name

Stand Up, Sit Down, page 3

1. up
2. up
3. down
4. up
5. down
6. up
7. down
8. up
9. down
10. up
11. up
12. up
13. down
14. up
15. up
16. down
17. up
18. down
19. up
20. down

End Action, page 3

1. clap
2. stomp
3. clap
4. stomp
5. clap
6. clap
7. stomp
8. stomp
9. clap
10. clap
11. stomp
12. clap
13. stomp
14. clap
15. stomp
16. clap

Find the Letter, page 4

G = green   B = blue
Y = yellow   O = orange
R = red

Aa Bb Cc Dd
Ee Ff Gg Hh
Ii Jj Kk Ll
Mm Nn Oo Pp
Qq Rr Ss Tt
Uu Vv Ww Xx
Yy Zz Name

Letter Sounds, page 6

G = green   B = blue
Br = brown   O = orange

Aa Bb Cc Dd
Ee Ff Gg Hh
Ii Jj Kk Ll
Mm Nn Oo Pp
Qq Rr Ss Tt
Uu Vv Ww Xx
Yy Zz

Write the Letter, page 7

(Drawings will vary.)

TLC10022 Copyright © Teaching & Learning Company, Carthage, IL 62321

Sentence Sounds, page 8
(Name at top of paper.)

2. 4: Keith, keeps, keys, pocket
3. 4: Sally, so, Sammy, Sarah
4. 6: Tim, Tina, get, into, town, today
5. 4: Now, Nick, needs, nickel
6. 4: Ruth, wrote, Rick, letter
7. 6: Monkeys, might, make, mess, my, room
8. 5: hope, Patty, pink, plum, pie
9. 4: Jack, Jill, jam, jelly
10. 3: Zip, buzz, blizzard
11. 4: Do, dance, red, dancing
12. 5: Find, Fatima, fell, off, roof

Picture This! page 9
(Name at top of paper.)

Long and Short, page 11
(Name at bottom of paper.)

Vowel Votes, page 13

a = 6 votes
e = 8 votes
i = 6 votes
(Name in the *e* column.)

___

i = 6 votes
o = 6 votes
u = 8 votes
(Name in the *u* column.)

Missing Vowels, page 14

(Name at top of paper.)

1. v_**e**_st	11. m_**u**_tt
2. st_**o**_p	12. b_**u**_n
3. st_**e**_p	13. y_**e**_t
4. sk_**i**_t	14. s_**a**_t
5. d_**a**_d	15. m_**o**_p
6. c_**u**_t	16. w_**e**_nt
7. d_**i**_d	17. t_**a**_n
8. c_**o**_t	18. k_**i**_n
9. sk_**i**_ll	19. h_**u**_t
10. p_**a**_t	20. t_**o**_p

Pre/Posttest, Part 2, page 16

1. Y
2. N
3. N
4. c.
5. b.
6. a.
7. b.
8. king
9. play
10. table

Is It Right? page 18

1. Y
2. N
3. N
4. Y
5. N
6. Y
7. N
8. Y
9. N
10. N
11. N
12. Y

Fluton's Follies, pages 19-20

G = green   B = blue
R = red   Y = yellow

Name

Three Choices, page 22

(Name in top right corner.)

1. big   eat   (dog)
2. run   stop   (house)
3. car   (sit)   no
4. (book)   red   went
5. (cake)   sun   get
6. good   cut   (go)
7. hat   (green)   and
8. (wet)   am   here
9. yellow   this   (well)
10. the   (class)   are
11. (blue)   blow   shoe
12. come   (read)   fun
13. me   store   (here)
14. (saw)   then   was

Scrambled Sense 1, page 25

1. apn   pan
2. gink   king
3. murd   drum
4. cpla   clap
5. figt   gift
6. etn   net
7. etn   ten
8. xif   fix
9. apm   map
10. lyap   play
11. dre   red
12. cpu   cup
13. bcka   back
14. pots   stop
15. Name

Scrambled Sense 2, page 26

1. sgnit   sting
2. sascl   class
3. shalsp   splash
4. bnchu   bunch
5. ctcha   catch
6. chrban   branch
7. knurt   trunk
8. colkc   clock
9. necilp   pencil
10. loyewl   yellow
11. gtehi   eight
12. blate   table
13. serho   horse
14. sihrt   shirt
15. dalsa   salad
       Name

Pre/Posttest, Part 3,

pages **27-28**

1. O
2. S
3. 2
4. top, bottom
5. black, white
6. 4: sliced, chopped, slit, carved
7. flour
8. rode
9. sale
10. stop
11. possible answers: eye, I
12. possible answers:
     unhappy, gloomy

Opal Opposite, page 29

Students should have found eight "backward" actions, indicated by italicized words in text of story. Pictures will vary.

Clap and Stomp, page 30

1. stomp
2. clap
3. clap
4. stomp
5. clap
6. clap
7. stomp
8. stomp
9. clap
10. stomp
11. clap
12. stomp
13. clap
14. clap
15. clap
16. stomp
17. stomp
18. stomp
19. stomp
20. stomp
21. clap
22. clap
23. stomp
24. clap

Hidden Opposites, page 31

1. up, down
2. short, tall
3. go, stop
4. freeze, thaw
5. wet, dry
6. top, bottom
7. end, beginning
8. heavy, light
9. hard, soft
10. sweet, sour
11. black, white
12. quickly, slowly
13. hate, love; lose, win
14. first, last; come, leave
15. Name

Synonym Stories, page 32

(Name at top of paper.)

1. 5: terrific, splendid, excellent, wonderful, super
2. 4: sliced, chopped, slit, carved
3. 3: high, towering, lofty
4. 5: soaked, soggy, drenched, damp, doused
5. 4: lie down, recline, relax, unwind
6. 6: soiled, grimy, filthy, grubby, dingy, unclean
7. 3: uproar, racket, din

Homonym Hay Day, page 34
(Name in top right corner.)

1. flower (flour)
2. (blew) blue
3. (doe) dough
4. four (for)
5. here (hear)
6. red (read)
7. (made) maid
8. road (rode)
9. (pair) pear
10. ate (eight)
11. night (knight)
12. know (no)
13. (sew) so
14. <u>to</u> (too) two
15. <u>their</u> there (they're)

Three's a Crowd, page 36
(Name at top of paper.)

1. write ~~right~~ left
2. ~~stop~~ go start
3. ~~dear~~ deer fawn
4. cents dime ~~sense~~
5. mad glad ~~angry~~
6. ~~meet~~ ham meat
7. new ~~old~~ knew
8. sail ~~sale~~ oar
9. quiet peace ~~piece~~
10. ~~cell~~ sell buy
11. tail tall ~~tale~~
12. one ~~won~~ two
13. sea see ~~ocean~~
14. bee ~~be~~ flea

Think! page 38
(Name at bottom of paper.)
Answers will vary.
Here are some possible outcomes:

1. hard
2. glad, excited
3. see, sea
4. down
5. small
6. dirty
7. I, eye
8. nice
9. loud
10. would, wood
11. light
12. silly
13. bottom
14. by, buy
15. unhappy, gloomy

Pre/Posttest, Part 4, page 39
(Name in top right corner.)

1. house, Jack
2. Answers will vary.
3. B.
4. A.
5. The (boy) <u>saw</u> the (fish)
6. Answers will vary.
7. Answers will vary.
8. verb
9. noun
10. 3: They, Pacific, Ocean

Animal Action, page 43
(Name at top of paper.)
Answers will vary.

1. A _____tiger_____ _____growls_____.
2. The _____duck_____ _____waddles_____.
3. A _____lion_____ _____eats_____.
4. Some _____deer_____ _____run_____.
5. A _____mule_____ _____sleeps_____.
6. The _____cow_____ _____moos_____.
7. My _____turtle_____ _____crawls_____.
8. The _____horse_____ _____neighs_____.
9. Some _____sheep_____ _____graze_____.
10. A _____rabbit_____ _____hops_____.

Not a Noun, page 44
(Name in top right corner.)

1. B.
2. C.
3. A.
4. C.
5. B.
6. C.
7. A.
8. C.
9. A.
10. C.
11. A.
12. B.
13. C.
14. A.
15. C.

Colored Sentences, page 46
G = green   B = blue
R = red

1. Ten yellow (fish) swam in a big (pond.)
    B   R   B
2. A young boy (dove) into the pond.
              R
3. He was very cold in the deep blue pond.
              G   G   G
4. The (boy) saw the (fish.)
     B   R   B
5. The (boy) grabbed the (fish.)
     B   R   B
6. They (swam) away.
        R
7. He walked out of the pond and dried himself.
     R   R
8. The boy (found) his fishing pole and (cast) it into
          R   R
   the pond.
9. The (fish) disappeared.
      B   R
10. The (sad)(little) boy walked to his (warm) home.
        G   G   B   G   B

Name

Sentence Building, pages 48-49
(Name in top right corner.)
Answers will vary greatly.
Here are some possible outcomes:

1. mouse
2. nibbles
3. A mouse nibbles.
4. A hungry mouse nibbles.
5. grandma
6. sews
7. The grandma sews.
8. The helpful grandma sews.
9. The helpful, happy grandma
   sews.

10. yard

11. was

12. The yard was

13. The yard was green.

14. clock

15. wiggle

16. shy

17. Yesterday I saw a <u>clock</u>. It could <u>wiggle</u>, and it was very <u>shy</u>.

Noun or Verb? pages 50-51
(Name in top left corner.)

1. verb
2. noun
3. noun
4. noun
5. verb
6. noun
7. noun
8. noun
9. verb
10. noun
11. noun
12. verb
13. verb
14. noun
15. noun
16. verb
17. noun
18. verb
19. verb
20. verb

Capital Sentences, page 52

1. 5: On, Saturday, Joshua, Elizabeth, Texas
2. 1: It
3. 3: They, Mississippi, River
4. 2: They, Austin
5. 3: Their, Dr., Smith
6. 3: If, Texas, May
7. 3: The, Maple, Street
8. 5: Mrs., Smith, Austin, Public, Library
9. 3: Another, Miltons, California
10. 3: They, American, Airlines
11. 2: Mrs., Milton
12. 3: They, Pacific, Ocean
13. Name

Pre/Posttest, Part 5,
pages 53-54
(Name in top right corner.)

1. yes
2. no
3. 3
4. 2
5. hen
6. come
7. done
8. B C D E
9. R S T U
10. My old cat Has a _____. (Answers will vary. Possibilities include: rat, bat, hat.)
11. B. rainbow
12. C. tree
13. B. over

Up and Down, page 55

1. stand	13. stand
2. stand	14. sit
3. stand	15. stand
4. sit	16. sit
5. sit	17. stand
6. stand	18. sit
7. sit	19. sit
8. sit	20. stand
9. stand	21. stand
10. sit	22. sit
11. sit	23. sit
12. stand	24. stand

Rows of Rhymes, page 56
(Name in top right corner.)

1. 4: cat, bat, that, rat
2. 3: big, gig, dig
3. 4: shawl, haul, ball, fall
4. 2: path, math
5. 3: must, just, rust
6. 5: king, ding, swing, bring, sling
7. 4: sash, cash, dash, bash
8. 3: bet, set, let
9. 5: mop, sop, cop, pop, hop
10. 4: Ben, Ken, pen, men
11. 4: bear, share, air, pair
12. 2: crib, rib

Rhyme Reasoning 1, page 57
(Name in top right corner.)

1.	bird	(hen)	when
2.	(red)	blue	said
3.	play	say	(sleigh)
4.	boo	(do)	clue
5.	bus	(done)	come
6.	crane	(brain)	heart
7.	(rose)	toes	tulip
8.	numb	hum	(jump)
9.	close	(shut)	nut
10.	(seat)	(greet)	(feet)
11.	(bean)	seen	plum
12.	funny	(shiny)	honey

Rhyme Reasoning 2, page 59
(Name in top right corner.)

1.	<u>bird</u>	hen	when
2.	red	<u>blue</u>	said
3.	<u>play</u>	say	sleigh
4.	boo	do	<u>clue</u>
5.	bus	done	<u>come</u>
6.	<u>crane</u>	brain	heart
7.	rose	<u>toes</u>	tulip
8.	numb	<u>hum</u>	jump
9.	close	shut	<u>nut</u>
10.	seat	<u>greet</u>	feet
11.	bean	seen	<u>plum</u>
12.	funny	shiny	<u>honey</u>

ABC–Listen! page 60

1. Name
2. J K L M
3. B C D E
4. R S T U
5. G H I J
6. O P Q
7. C D E F G
8. S T U V W
9. F G H I J
10. L M N O P
11. N O P Q

Dictated Rhymes, page 61

(Name at top of paper.)
Outcomes will vary.
Possible words to complete each rhyme are given here.

2. rat, hat, bat
3. play, pay, pray
4. beet, meat, treat
5. pen, wren, hen
6. toad, load
7. wheel, seal, eel
8. tie, fly
9. box
10. fan, pan, man

Haiku, pages 62-63

(Name at top of paper.)

1. B. blizzard
2. A. zebra
3. C. tree
4. B. sun
5. C. waterfall
6. A. dog
7. B. fall
8. A. desert
9. C. rose
10. B. caterpillar

Limerick Lessons, pages 64-65

(Name at top of paper.)

1. A. over
2. C. confetti
3. A. took
4. C. honey
5. A. peeling
6. B. still
7. A. cloud
8. B. brick
9. C. mush
10. B. lark

Pre/Posttest, Part 6, page 67

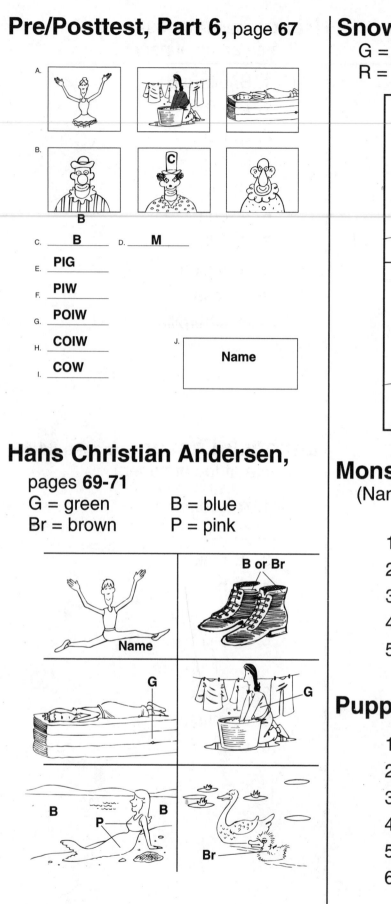

A.

B.

C. **B**   D. **M**

E. **PIG**

F. **PIW**

G. **POIW**

H. **COIW**

I. **COW**

J.

Name

Hans Christian Andersen, pages **69-71**

G = green   B = blue

Br = brown   P = pink

B or Br

Name

G

G

B   B

P

Br

Snowmen, page 72

G = green   B = blue

R = red

G

B

B

Name — B

Monster Monkey, pages 74-75

(Name in top left corner.)

1. M   6. 2

2. B   7. L

3. B   8. T

4. J   9. C

5. G   10. B

Puppy Love, page 76

1. PUPPY   7. GPDOP

2. PUPOPY   8. GPDO

3. UPOPY   9. GDO

4. UPDOPY   10. DOG

5. UPDOP   11. Name

6. GUPDOP

TLC10022 Copyright © Teaching & Learning Company, Carthage, IL 62321